M000015233

FOOTSTEPS IN THE ATTIC

PAUL F. ENO

Copyright ©2002 by Paul F. Eno
All rights reserved
Unless otherwise noted

Published by
New River Press
645 Fairmount Street
Woonsocket, R.I.02895
(800) 244-1257
www.NewRiverPress.com

Printed in Canada

ISBN 1-891724-02-9

Cover Photo by Shane Sirois

To my mother,
who gave up everything for me.

CONTENTS

CONTENTS

*Most names in the case histories recounted in this book have
been changed to protect the anonymity of those involved.*

Footsteps in the Attic

INTRODUCTION: WHAT ARE GHOSTS?

Physics, anyone?

What do you say when someone asks when and where were you born? You reply quite untruthfully that you were born in such and such a place in this or that year. In fact, you were born out of eternal blackness some seventeen billion years ago in an unimaginable blast of light, the primal explosion that hurled a storm of matter and antimatter in directions that hadn't even existed until that instant. Reeling outward at nearly the speed of light was the stuff that would become quasars and galaxies, planets and oceans, mountains and trees — and you.

After more than thirty years investigating ghosts, I'm convinced that it's to this first split-second of Creation that we must look to begin to understand what they are. That's because matter and antimatter weren't all that were created at the Creation. Space and time also had their origins at that instant in what physicists call a "space-time foam."

It was pioneers among these scientists, legendary people like Albert Einstein, Neils Bohr and Werner Heisenberg, who began in the early twentieth century to rediscover that matter is just another form of energy, that time as we understand it is an illusion, and that space and time are one and the same. And as scientific equipment and experimentation have become more sophisticated, reality's weirdness has become more and more glaring.

Among the more crucial findings of modern physics

that I feel can help explain ghosts, poltergeists, extrasensory perception (ESP) and the rest of what we call paranormal:

• Throughout modern history, atoms have been thought of as the "building blocks" of matter, but apparently they — and matter — are just energy.

• Subatomic (smaller than atoms) particles, or "wavicles" as they're called because they're only particles sometimes, usually spread out as energy waves, sometimes across vast distances in what is referred to as "space-time." These waves only "collapse" and turn into particles when somebody looks at them....

• Certain "wavicles" travel back and forth across space-time, often producing an effect *before* the cause that created the effect. Can this help explain clairvoyance, clairaudience and other experiences of "seeing the future" or, as in *déjà vu*, the "past"?

• When someone observes a wavicle, thereby "collapsing the wave function," as physicists say, and changing the energy wave into a particle, this makes the particle "real," as it were. Could this mean that we create, or at least profoundly influence, the reality around us? Is this how we "connect" with ghosts?

• Wavicles can disappear from one place and appear in another, sometimes vast distances away, *without traversing the space in between.* Does this indicate that they are traveling through "parallel universes," a critical theory of my own when interpreting ghosts?

• Wavicles seem to "communicate" and interact with each other across incredible distances with no apparent means of doing so. The Alain Aspect Experiment proves it. Can this help explain ESP, "distant viewing" and "visitation apparitions"?

Because those working in the branch of physics known as quantum mechanics have discovered much of this, we refer to this scheme of things as "quantum reality." And as we travel though the case studies in this book, I hope that the immediacy of quantum reality will become clear.

We're the primitives!

I say that science is "rediscovering" all this because it already seems to be part of the vision found in so-called primitive cultures and religions. That's why this "new physics" has prompted numerous books about how ancient faiths and world views often mesh uncannily with quantum reality.

In fact, it's becoming plain that we in Western culture have been the philosophical freaks of human history. We long ago rejected the holistic sciences of the ancients and the "primitives" only to find today that our materialistic science just isn't up to the job because it does little to explain either consciousness or the human experience. After centuries of unsuccessfully trying to make science fit a model that says everything, even consciousness, is based on matter, we have succeeded only in creating intellectual confusion. This kind of science, known in philosophy as "scientific materialism" or "material realism," is a pitifully incomplete picture of the universe. It has emasculated our spirituality, disenchanted our everyday lives, hobbled our sense of community and left us by the roadside as lonely (albeit well fed) "consumers." And the current states of our planet, our society and many of our lives bitterly prove the point.

Whence ghosts?

In quantum reality, all of us, whether "living" or "dead," are intimately united in very concrete ways. Time as we understand it doesn't exist. Our sense of "self" is an illusion. All that ever was and all that ever can be exists all at once — in multiple, parallel universes.

This concept of parallel universes, known as the "multiverse," is no joke. It's becoming widely accepted among scientists, who already use it to advance practical fields such as computing. Among the leading advocates of this interpretation of quantum mechanics is Oxford University physicist David Deutsch, who believes we can reach into other universes and use them to improve our own!

The multiverse is becoming less of a theory and more of a fact with each passing month, and you can expect astounding things to come of it.

The multiverse apparently is shot through with consciousness. It contains all outcomes, possibilities and creatures. Take two given parallel universes, and the only difference between them could be that in one you exist and in the other you don't. Take two other parallel universes, and the differences may be so far-reaching that the worlds and beings in one would be unrecognizable to beings from the other.

Despite Hollywood's canted portrayal of this in science-fiction shows like *Sliders* or *Quantum Leap,* these universes don't seem to be separate as much as they are contiguous and sometimes even coexistent. Parallel universes often are referred to popularly as "other dimensions."

Remember the physicists' idea of a "space-time foam" born at the Creation? Picture this foam as soap bubbles in a bathtub: The bubbles, each of which is a universe, are crowded together, sliding against one another and passing through one another frequently — *with contact and even interaction in unexpected places and times.* Indeed, space-time seems to be full of ripples, holes, currents, cross-rips and eddies, rather like a river that we spend all eternity swimming in.

I hasten to add that, while all physicists acknowledge this multiple worlds interpretation (MWI) of quantum mechanics, only about fifty-eight percent believe it, according to a 1995 study by BLTC Research. So the MWI, which originated in a 1957 Princeton doctoral dissertation by one Hugh Everett III, still isn't universally accepted. And those who do accept it often vary considerably in how they interpret it. Some say that parallel universes aren't "complete" and consist only of "unrealized" people and things.

It seems to me that the crux of the MWI skeptics' argument is: Sure, it's undeniable that sheer fantasy seems to rule at the subatomic level, but how can this have any affect on reality at the level of planets, mountains, people and grasshoppers? I ask in response that if everything we see, feel and know is built on this subatomic wonderland, how can there *not* be macroscopic effects?

I believe I've seen these effects vividly as a paranormal investigator, and I further believe that because the force we call electromagnetism is the basis of everything at the subatomic level, it's the prime factor on our own level of quantum reality too.

While many physicists quite understandably fume over people like me, non-scientists who "take quantum mechanics and run with it," I challenge any of them to come up with a better explanation for the paranormal phenomena I have witnessed for decades. After all, scientists and philosophers often cite the principle known as "Ockham's Razor" or the "Principle of Parsimony": The simplest or most obvious explanation usually is the correct one.

So we apparently live not just in the universe but in the multiverse. And lifeforms great and small, "normal" and "weird" are beside us forever, whether we know it or not. Combine all this with its implications for human consciousness, and we finally might discover the answer to the question "What are ghosts?"

Quantum mechanics points to the mind-wrenching idea that our consciousness isn't inside us: It's "non-local" or shared. Our consciousness and all consciousnesses sweep across space-time in immeasurable waves. Where these waves intersect, those are the people, places and things we know. Where they form bonds, those are the people, places and things we love, have loved and will love in our lives. But where there is an aware connection between our consciousness and that of someone – whether a human or non-human someone – from another part of the multiverse – those are what we know as ghosts. It's at these cosmic conjunctions that ghost experiences happen *not only for us but for the being with whose consciousness we have connected.*

The further implication is that there really is no such thing as death: Your consciousness, even your body, is always alive at all sorts of times and places in the multiverse. Taken to its furthest point, it could mean that, all factors considered, you share your consciousness with everyone who ever was and ever will be -- everywhere in the multiverse.

Goodbye to the séance room

I'm sure you can see how this changes everything, especially the naïve, one-dimensional, séance-room view of what ghosts are. I don't believe that ghosts are "spirits of the dead" because I don't believe in death. In the multiverse, once you're possible, you exist. And once you exist, you exist forever one way or another. Besides, death is the absence of life, and the ghosts I've met are very much alive. What we call ghosts are lifeforms just as you and I are. I certainly don't believe that ghosts are just video-like "recordings" on the environment. Many parapsychologists suggest this for lack of any better explanation and because they don't take quantum reality seriously enough.

My experience is that there are three basic phenomena that people experience as ghosts: space-time displacements, parasites and what traditionally are known as visitation apparitions. For any of these to become apparent to an observer, electrical and geomagnetic factors (sometimes called "earth energies") that affect quantum reality have to fall into place. These include the electro-magnetic fields at a given site, the minerals in the soil, the height of the water table, and even the proximity of high-tension wires. Because we, too, run on electricity (our brains and muscles work through electrical impulses), we have "bioelectric" fields around our bodies (occultists refer to these are "auras") and we're rather literally wired into the whole electrical scheme of the multiverse. As a matter of fact, we, and all mammals, emit a static DC electrical field, which easily interacts with other electrical and magnetic fields.

Adding to this electrical menagerie, I find that paranormal phenomena tend to center around indoor areas where there is plumbing, such as kitchens and bathrooms. Water, of course, is one of the best conductors of electricity. Going even further, I find that phenomena seem to draw power from a building's electrical system: In my first interview during a typical case, residents usually tell me that at least some phenomena have centered on appliances, especially television sets, audio equipment, microwave ovens and refrigerators. I always ask if there has been an increase in the electric bill since phenomena began and, once people check, I'm very surprised if I don't get a big "yes!"

The psychic, psychiatric and physical states of the observer(s), and even the plumbing and wiring of their "haunted" buildings, are crucial to whether or not phenomena occur and are perceived. In other words, you have to be wired into a phenomenon in order to experience it.

Also relevant at any haunted site is what might be happening there in other parts of space-time that we would refer to as the "past" or the "future." If murder is committed in a house, for example, that highly charged act and the trauma it causes people send out ripples through space-time. People in other areas of space-time, if they

Footsteps in the Attic

are electrically "tuned" in and are in the right place at the right time, may encounter these ripples. These might produce anything from vague impressions of fear to vivid visions of the murders, especially if those perceiving them happen to live on or near the physical spot where it's occurring "elsewhen." It might involve feelings of sympathy, empathy and even rudimentary contact with the people who were or will be going through the experience.

If the event hasn't happened yet (in our part of the multiverse) and someone is sensitive enough, he or she can indeed pick up the ripples that have gone "backward" in space-time. This, of course, is what we commonly refer to as a premonition or precognitive (clairvoyant) experience.

So if the people, the place and the electromagnetic "chemistry" are just right, the result quite literally can be a haunted house or, at least, a very bizarre experience.

Hold on a minute....

Before shouting, "Ahhhh Haaaa! We have a ghost!" I need to point out that seeing and hearing things can have psychiatric or neural explanations, namely as symptoms of schizophrenia, schizotypal personality disorder (SPD) or temporal-lobe epilepsy (TLE).

TLE is especially interesting. It can create religious fanatics, cause altered states of consciousness that include vivid religious imagery and schizophrenia-like states. It may involve mood disorders, aggression and clinical depression. It also can cause frequent subjective paranormal experiences, including telepathy, mediumistic trances, automatic writing, experiences of presences or of lights and colors around people, and out-of body experiences. It also can contribute to artistic creativity and spiritual leadership. Today, people like Edgar Allan Poe and Joan of Arc might be diagnosed with TLE.

Footsteps in the Attic

The trouble from my point of view is that many psychiatrists diagnose TLE *just because a person has paranormal experiences* and may happen to be a little flaky. I saw this often while doing field work in psychiatric hospitals as a student. This approach can be a big mistake because it implies that spiritual and paranormal experiences can't be real.

Just suppose that TLE and conditions like it don't *cause* people to have paranormal experiences. Suppose they *allow* people to have them by expanding their awareness of wider areas of space-time. What if they wrench open the long-stuck door to the primal psychic abilities the so-called primitives say we all had when we had to live by our wits as hunter-gatherers? Further, what if dissociative identity disorder (multiple personalities) isn't a disorder at all, but a state of heightened awareness in which "the patient" is in touch with who he or she is in one or more parallel universes?

Whatever the case, to find out will take serious research by open-minded people far more competent than I. I'm not a doctor and don't take it upon myself to diagnose anything when I'm on a case. I have a strict policy: When deciding whether to pursue a case as paranormal or to contact a psychiatrist who consults for my investigative team, I look for multiple witnesses to the paranormal experiences. One of the first questions I ask is, "Who else is seeing or hearing all this?"

And, interestingly, the first question almost everyone asks me is, "Do you think we're crazy?"

A breakthrough

In the April 1998 *Journal of the Society for Psychical Research,* British investigators reported an especially important finding: Very low frequency (VLF) sound waves, also known as "infra-sound," can literally become trapped in buildings and produce some of the basic phenomena traditionally associated with ghosts. As "standing waves," these VLFs can stimulate feelings of fear and cold, produce minor poltergeist activity and even your basic apparition. VLF sounds are inaudible to humans but can be picked up by some animals, such as dogs and horses, long celebrated as the self-appointed psychic detectives of the animal kingdom.

Standing waves can be caused by anything from the wind passing over a house to a malfunctioning refrigerator fan to the subwoofers on a stereo system. Since this is a relatively new discovery and I as yet have no sophisticated equipment for detecting VLFs, I usually end up unplugging various appliances in a process of elimination to help determine if there are standing waves involved.

Over the years, I've dealt with many outdoor cases, such as "Connecticut's Village of Voices," (*Faces at the Window*, New River Press, 1998). I can well imagine some version of the standing-wave phenomenon transferred to an outdoor setting. One clue might be the "Taos hum" oddity: An unexplained, low-frequency sound heard in various places around the world, especially in the Northern Hemisphere. The "hum" has been described as similar to the sound of a diesel truck idling some distance away. Scientists believe it could be seismic in origin.

I'll go no further into geotechnics, torsion physics, dark matter, subtle energies, the super spectrum hypothesis or propagating fields, but I will say that acquiring a VLF antenna and checking "Taos hum" areas for reports of paranormal activity are on my "list of things to do."

Ghosts from elsewhen

After I've made sure that my subjects aren't nuts, that their houses aren't full of standing waves and that Mother Earth isn't humming merrily away under their feet, I start looking at the more bizarre quantum possibilities.

What I call "ghosts from elsewhen" essentially are conscious glimpses into other areas of space-time. As long as the electromagnetic "ducks are in line," these space-time displacements can happen to anyone, anytime, anywhere. I believe they occur at points where two or more universes overlap. They range from the appearance or disappearance of everyday items (or even people) all the way to voices and apparitions of things, places, animals and people of what to us would be the past, future or simply a very different world. This is why people report not only ghosts of the so-called dead, but of those who are "still alive," along with phantom objects, animals, buildings and even whole towns. Some people even report seeing ghosts of themselves!

The translucent old lady who glides down your stairway at midnight every other Wednesday and vanishes through the front door almost certainly is a space-time displacement: a glimpse into a corner of the multiverse where your past — or future — is her present. Under the right circumstances, as we'll see from some of our case studies, we can interact with people, places and things from other times. Imagine the implications for historians and genealogists!

In my experience, space-time displacements explain many ghosts and a number of other everyday paranormal phenomena, some of which we might not even notice.

Parasites

When a ghostly experience goes beyond the occasional sighting of somebody or something from somewhere or somewhen else, we could be looking at real trouble. Over the years, I often have run up against what I can describe only as parasitic, extradimensional lifeforms. These seem to use electromagnetic fields, including the bioelectric fields around our bodies, to gain access to where we are so they can feed off our energy. I believe that many of them can slip from one universe to another. I'm not sure whether these lifeforms are native to our corner of space-time or whether they come from some other part of the multiverse.

Among other phenomena, I believe these parasites include poltergeists (see glossary). They demonstrate intelligence and have a remarkable ability to learn, often causing apparitions and voice phenomena. They seem particularly drawn to people who have "been through the mill" in their lives and remain in a vulnerable state spiritually and psychologically, pumping out negative energy upon which the parasites seem to feed.

When seemingly innocent phenomena start small and steadily worsen, when you or your family members begin feeling threatened and fearful because of what's going on, or when something starts playing Frisbee with your fine china, it's a pretty good bet that you're playing host to one of these parasites. And be assured that they are *not* your friends. As a matter of fact, I have no doubt whatever that parasites are the basis for the evil spirits and demons known in all cultures.

I include "tulpas" in my list of parasites. Known in many cultures and prominent among the darker spiritual concepts of the Tibetan Buddhists, the tulpa is believed to be a spirit deliberately created by concentration. Many tulpas are well documented, and I have cases in my files about groups of parapsychology students who actually have "created" tulpas. These things often take on lives of their own and can be very difficult to "put away." Some have even been photographed. Personally, I believe that tulpas are parasites, or some other sort of extradimensional entity, that already exist and just use the opportunity to take form and gain strength through all the human concentration.

Tulpas don't always have a humanoid appearance. I've

Footsteps in the Attic

had a number of cases in which people would hear animal-like snarling, see red eyes peering at them from under furniture or endure apparitions of bizarre animals. I believe these are parasites because, once I teach the victims to take control of their own emotions and of the situation with positive energy, the phenomena always stop.

'Skyfish'

I strongly suspect that there are other lifeforms that we know little or nothing about that might be around us all the time. These include the fascinating "skyfish" or "rods." Hailing from one of the more obscure corners of cryptozoology (the study of mysterious, unofficial animals, such as Bigfoot), skyfish appear to be long, narrow, fast-moving creatures that live in the air. From four inches to a few feet long, they crop up now and again in photos, which sometimes are detailed enough to show sets of small wings or fins along their bodies.

If they actually exist, I have little doubt that skyfish, which appear to be completely harmless, are responsible for many a supposed paranormal photo and perhaps some phenomena, too. I'm sure that if one or more get into a house, there can be some uproarious goings-on!

The good with the bad

I stress that there are lifeforms and there are lifeforms. We ourselves are lifeforms living among the universes of quantum reality, and some of us are fine specimens of humanity while others are nitwits. There seem to be plenty of other kinds of lifeforms around us, many neutral like the theoretical skyfish, and I'm certain that occasional encounters with them throughout history have been responsible for the stories of angels, fairies, elves, leprechauns, space aliens or what have you. And who knows what "legends" our own antics may have spawned "elsewhere" or "elsewhen."

As any experienced shaman will tell you, some of these lifeforms may be in a position in the multiverse to help us in some way, perhaps for the same reason that some people dedicate their lives to helping animals, or simply from a spirit of selfless love. We've all felt loving presences at one point or another in our lives. It's when the parasites arrive that trouble begins.

The diagnostic problem is that, with the right factors present, several kinds of ghosts can manifest in the same place and not necessarily be related to one another. With the right energies at a site, there could be space-time displacements. Add the right (or wrong) kind of people and the same energies, and parasites can manifest. Things can become a real mess.

Deathless love

Finally, I believe that there are legitimate visitation apparitions, often from loved ones who have "moved on." It may sound hokey or unscientific, but I can't come to any other conclusion: There seem to be some universes or states of awareness that are clearer or more enlightened than ours. Those whose condition puts their consciousness in one of these universes after their "deaths" in our corner of quantum reality seem to be able to aid loved ones and others who remain. The many cultures that honor their ancestors don't do so for nothing.

How I investigate

As you can guess, I investigate haunted places a little differently than do most researchers. People usually contact me about paranormal problems after they read something I've written, or they approach me after a lecture or book signing. I'll get the bare necessities of someone's story and decide if it's worth investigating further. I don't let people tell me more than what I absolutely need to know before my first visit, which I almost always make alone.

My first step on arrival is to ask people to sign a paper that reserves to me the rights to all recordings and photos taken at the site. Since I don't charge for investigations, that sometimes helps me recoup when I write or lecture about the case later. In the same paper, I guarantee that I won't use the people's real names unless they grant permission in writing. And after my experience in the Bridgeport poltergeist case of 1974 (see *Faces at the Window*, New River Press, 1998), people can be sure that I make every effort to keep the press out of it!

I examine the site completely. If it's a house, I check the whole property for impressions, inside and out. Most ghost hunters don't check the property around a house for energy, and that's a mistake because it's a source of crucial electromagnetic clues. I take some magnetic-field readings and form some impressions. I'm not playing psychic, I'm looking for electrical fields, cold spots and other clues that I've learned about from experience.

Only after that will I do my first in-depth interview with the family or other witnesses.

I also rely a great deal on photography. Because of the electromagnetics of the paranormal, phenomena often manifest on film or digital media as everything from orbs of light and fogs to faces and entire figures. Of course, with today's computers, photo fakery is a piece of cake. So I'm paranoid about photos: Unless I or one of my hand-picked team members have taken them, I don't trust them. Even then, each photo is vetted by at least two photography experts (usually with computer analysis) before being dubbed with the qualified label "anomalous."

I pay close attention to animals that live at the site, especially family pets that may have a psychic bond with whomever lives there. Many species, including dogs and cats, can see and hear in ranges we can't. They don't lie and they don't stage hoaxes. How they react to their environment can be one clue to whether or not a situation is paranormal.

People often ask me about electronic voice phenomena (EVP)(see glossary). As a rule, I don't rely on it. I don't trust it because there are all sorts of electronic explanations for it, most of them non-paranormal.

How do we see ghosts?

I'm often asked two questions: How do we see ghosts and how do they get recorded on film or by a digital photographic device? I believe both questions have the same answer. Our eyes can pick up only certain light spectra. Cameras can pick up those and more. Among these spectra are those produced by some forms of plasma. Plasma, the most common form of matter/energy in the universe, is really just electrified air molecules.

Plasma can be strengthened and controlled by the very electromagnetic fields I believe are at the root of our paranormal experiences. I believe that when we see ghostly phenomena, with our eyes or with a camera, they are manifesting as plasma of one kind or another.

The next steps

If what witnesses tell me jives with what I see as an investigation progresses, I'll look for evidence of human issues that might be connecting with and feeding the phenomena, such as family dysfunction. This can get complicated. For example, if a father shows me bruises on his children and says they're caused by a poltergeist, I start looking for the phone number of the state's family-services agency.

If I do think something legitimately paranormal is going on, I'll usually bring in one or more members of my investigative team. This group changes over the years but these days includes a soil engineer, an electrical engineer, an expert in the literature of death and dying, a psychiatrist and several photography experts. I also work with my good friend and "heir apparent" in this field, Shane Sirois of New Hampshire, known as Silent Bear, a Blackfoot medicine man.

All together, these experts can help me pin down everything from a site's soil composition and water-table level to the psychiatric states of the people experiencing the phenomena and the nature of the entities, if any, causing it. Most importantly, they sometimes see factors that I miss and point out alternatives I haven't considered.

Very occasionally I'll call in clergy from whatever religion the people belong to. But I've learned to be careful with men and women of the cloth: Contrary to popular belief, they are very seldom trained in how to deal with paranormal phenomena. Many will do nothing and some will do more harm than good. Most who are knowledgeable tend, not surprisingly, to have theological presuppositions. Still, the right clergy can be invaluable in calming and reassuring victims of the more negative phenomena, and that in itself can help defuse the situation.

What, no psychics?

I seldom if ever work with psychics. With a few rare exceptions, I find them absolutely ridiculous. In my experience at least, and excepting the very few good ones I've met over the years, most psychics seem to be on an ego trip, with little understanding of what their often legitimate sensitivities actually mean. And almost all of them are fixated on the nineteenth century, séance-room vision of what this is all about.

The fact is that everyone is psychic to some degree. It's one of the prime survival mechanisms we inherit from our hunter-gatherer ancestors. If that weren't so, we'd never have "feelings" of danger or of being watched. We'd never have "hunches" or have a clue what other people are thinking. I sometimes use the Christmas-light analogy. In a way, humanity is like a string of lights. Each of us is a bulb with its own light, but we share the same power source, which in turn is connected to a vast grid that corresponds to the multiverse.

We are very much in touch with each other and the multiverse. Indeed, humanity and the multiverse are truly one in ways that our imaginations are powerless to grasp — yet. Indeed, we're a very young species, and it's the first day of school.

Paul F. Eno
Town's End
2001

Footsteps in the Attic

I

GHOSTS FROM ELSEWHEN

Footsteps in the Attic

Think back. How often has it happened? You're puttering along on your way to work. Suddenly, you get that funny, half-threatening feeling that somebody is too close. Glancing in the rear-view mirror, you see some cowboy ready to drive through your tailgate. Steaming, you check the road ahead, tighten the grip on the steering wheel and promise yourself that you won't speed up. Then your eyes zip back to the mirror.

The cowboy has vanished. He didn't pass you, and there's nowhere he could have turned. You puzzle about this, and the memory stays with you for part of your day. You don't tell people about the experience because you don't want them to think you're weird. But soon the Western mind's hunger of rationality kicks in, you chalk up the event as "one of those things" and forget about it.

Perhaps you're right. Maybe the guy veered off into some road you've never noticed. But perhaps you're wrong. Maybe this was one of those hundreds of odd little incidents that we shrug off throughout our daily lives: Household items that don't stay where we put them, strangers who seem to appear and disappear, even streets or buildings that prompt a wrinkled brow and the thought, "I never noticed that before!"

Of course, the vast majority of these incidents probably result from inattention or forgetfulness on our part. That's certainly true as we age and experience more and more (as I'll politely call them) "senior moments." Many people, especially older folks, also experience what's known in psychology as confabulation, the unconscious combining of real memory segments into entirely new, but false, memories.

Nevertheless, some of these bizarre, day-to-day happenings seem to defy day-to-day explanations, and they could well be our own little experiences of quantum reality. Slips in time. Displacements in space. Tiny conjunctions of parallel worlds.

Footsteps in the Attic

Something About Hats

The Restless Fedora

"I'm almost embarrassed to ask this," my companion muttered as we left our psychology class. "It's about my uncle's hat."

It was late 1977, and we were graduate students at Trinity College in Hartford, Connecticut. I was rounding out my seventh year as a paranormal investigator, had recently made my first television appearance and knew what was coming.

"Your uncle's what?" I asked.

"Well, his hat. It keeps moving. I know you're into this stuff, so I thought I'd ask you," my fellow student replied.

"Is he dead?"

"My uncle? Not yet. If it's a ghost, it's not him."

Today, given what I've already said about the multiverse, I would have responded: "Not necessarily!"

A week later I interviewed this chap, a charming, seventy-two year-old gentleman named Sean Brannon who had emigrated from Ireland a half century before. He lived with his wife, Betty, in a small, well kept house in the Town of Wethersfield, just south of Hartford. With my passion for New England history, the house, built in the eighteenth century, was glorious, with an ancient fireplace, some original fixtures and other antiquarian delights.

At this point, you're probably going, "AAH HAAAH! An old house. Therefore GHOSTS!"

A house's age isn't a "dead" giveaway. Sure, an old house is likely to have had lots of tenants, with a greater chance of something big having happened to send out ripples into space-time that could come back to haunt residents. But whether weird stuff happens in an old house depends just as much on the site's electromagnetic fields, the house's past — and future — and the kind of people who live there.

In any case, our hat in question was a fedora that had been Sean's trademark for years. Having seen better days, it had been replaced by Santa the previous Christmas. Uncle Sean now sported a new felt lid whenever he ventured beyond his quaint doorstep. The old fedora, however, apparently had taken umbrage at being retired. The hoary *chapeau* kept reappearing on the clothes hook by the back door, where it had hung every night during its long tenure.

"And wouldn't ya know, I couldn't bring meself to throw it away. I just put it in me closet," the little, white-haired fellow told me in his charming brogue. "And back on its old hook by the door it'd be every bloody mornin'!"

After speculating seriously about leprechauns (no kidding), he asked about ghosts.

"Do any other odd things happen in the house?" I asked.

"Nothin' ya wouldn't expect."

"What would I expect, Mr. Brannon?"

"Ya'ave to realize, Mr. Ayno, ghosts are as thick as molasses in Ireland, so nobody pays any attention to 'em. I'd just like the bloody hat to stay where I put it. There's only so many hooks by the door, ya know!"

I couldn't get a straight answer out of him.

"Have you or Mrs. Brannon seen the hat appear, disappear or move through the air?"

"Well, we never really looked!" was the frustrating reply.

After a great deal more of this ambiguous conversation, I gathered that there were no particular phenomena that would suggest an actual haunting. None of those "cold spots" ghosts are famous for. No poltergeists rearranging the Brannons' furniture. No footsteps in the attic. I thoroughly checked all the rooms and got no clear

Footsteps in the Attic

feeling of paranormal activity, which always has manifested to me as sharp tingles on the skin produced, as I believe, by the electrical fields associated with these entities.

In 1977, I could give dear old Sean no concrete explanation for his hat's antics. But if I'd known then what I know now, it would have been relatively easy.

"Mr. Brannon," I could have said. "Through the miracle of quantum mechanics, you are haunting your own house." I would have put it somewhat more discreetly, of course, but that's it in a nutshell.

We, aided by our little routines and daily habits, apparently make repetitive paths in space-time. In other words, the more we do something, the more parallel universes it happens in. Couple this with the fact that all physical objects, such as ourselves and our hats, make their own little "warps" or "holes" in space-time because of the tiny gravitational fields they produce, and we can begin to come up with a better explanation than leprechauns.

In my opinion, Sean over the years had set up such a pattern with his hat habit that the hat kept slipping in and out of its own little hole in space-time even after the old sweetheart stopped the routine. The myriad universes in which Sean still wore the fedora and replaced it on its hook each night were converging in the house in just the right way that the hat appeared to keep up the old routine!

As I said in the introduction to this book, such phenomena are essentially electrical. Had I known enough in those days to investigate the land under the house as well as the house itself, I can pretty well guarantee that I would have found natural electromagnetic fields of an intensity to feed such minor phenomena. Had the "chemistry" of the situation been slightly different, if the electromagnetic fields were stronger or Sean or Betty more attuned to them, they easily might have seen a phantom Sean replacing that hat on its hook every night: truly a ghost from elsewhen. And even as it was, I think that if I'd spent the night near that hat hook by the back door, I'd definitely have felt the paranormal presence of a very "otherworldly" Sean as the old fedora reappeared.

The disappearing cap

Some years later, after I'd married my long-suffering wife and we'd had our first child, I had my own hat experience.

It was the cold winter of 1985-1986, and our two year-old son, Jonathan, loved to spend time outside in our wooded hollow in Cumberland, Rhode Island. One windy afternoon I was dressing him for an excursion, and I went to his room for his navy-blue knit cap. I found it in its usual place and picked it up. Then I dropped it — right at my feet.

When I looked down, however, the cap was nowhere to be seen. Several searches of the small room revealed nothing, and Jonathan had to be content with a fur hat with ear flaps. In the following days, more searches brought forth no cap, and we finally surrendered the wayward headgear to its mysterious fate.

Nearly five weeks later I was in Jonathan's room when I happened to glance at the floor. There, on the very spot I'd dropped it over a month before, was the cap, back from wherever it had been.

"Thanks a lot," I muttered. "It's spring."

The Haunter

I used to think "the haunter" was what scholars refer to as an "urban legend," a story that started somewhere, then got repeated, changed and exaggerated to the point that it joined the fabric of modern folklore. Alligators in the sewers, the exotic rat or wombat that gets adopted because some schmuck thinks it's a Chihuahua, and the elephant that sits on the Volkswagen are among thousands of popular urban legends.

I thought "the haunter" was one of these until I ran into one myself.

October 1978 was remarkably warm in southern New England. I was living alone in a writer's paradise: a virtually neighborless little house on the shores of quiet Shenipsit Lake in Tolland, Connecticut.

My work as a paranormal investigator was chugging along but, fresh out of graduate school, my career as a journalist hadn't really begun. There's little or no money in ghosts unless one is a charlatan, a showman or both. So I was supporting myself by writing, believe it or not, plays for producer Akiva Talmi and the Connecticut Dance Theater, and by moonlighting as a chimney sweep!

On one of these paranormally warm days, I was ensconced on my back porch, sweating over a scene in which I was supposed to get five ballet dancers, five puppets and a flock of fake butterflies from one side of the stage to the other. I was gazing out at the lake, picturing the whole mob in a tangled heap at stage center, when I was saved by the telephone.

It was a very worried young woman.

"I'm sorry to bother you with this, but I know my sister and she isn't crazy," the caller, Janice DeVito, said after the preliminaries.

It seemed that Janice and her older sister, Patricia, both students at the nearby University of Connecticut, had spent a few days with their boyfriends in southern Maine a few weekends before. There, the four of them had a scare that would haunt them for the rest of their lives, I was told.

This is how Jan recounted it.

"Pat has always been big on reincarnation, dreams and *déjà vu*. Every now and then, we'll be someplace and she'll come out with something about this or that being familiar," she explained.

"We were driving down this old road in Maine when Pat suddenly screamed. She scared the (fecal matter) out of us! 'Stop! Stop!' she yelled. Joey (Janice's boyfriend) was driving, and he hit the brakes."

Pat was "white as a ghost," Jan said.

"Pat yelled, 'Oh, my God!' and pointed at this house maybe a hundred feet back from the road."

Everybody's skin was crawling by this time, according to Jan, who noted that the house was white, only about ten years old and had a rather neglected yard.

"I know this house! This is my house!" Pat yelled, leaping out of the car.

Terrified, and convinced that her sister finally had "lost it," Jan and the boys tore after her but didn't catch up until she had pounded on the front door. The door opened just as the trio was trying to pull Pat away.

Jan told me that what happened next would be seared into her memory "until the day I die."

The woman who answered the door was in her mid-thirties. She took one look at Pat, screamed and went stumbling back into the house. A slightly older man then appeared, gaped at Pat, but was unable to speak.

In the meantime, Pat had recovered somewhat, apologized and started to explain her feeling that she knew the house. The woman "was still shaking like a leaf," Jan recalled, but the man, as pale as ever, finally found his voice.

Footsteps in the Attic

"I...I wouldn't be surprised if you did know this house," he blurted. "It's you! It's haunted by you! For God's sake, please go!"

Even with that, the man and woman continued to stare at Pat in fascination, seeming almost reluctant to shut the door.

Joey took charge.

"We're sorry to have bothered you," he said, pulling the others away and down the path to the car. Even as they drove away, the coupled continued to gaze at them from their front door.

"We never found out what it was all about, but it was scary as hell," Jan concluded. "Pat's been depressed and scared ever since."

Needless to say, this case captured my imagination. The first thing I did was interview Pat, on October 20. She claimed that she had been dreaming about this house for at least a year. Interestingly, the dreams had stopped as soon as she actually encountered the place, she said.

"There were a couple of different dreams about my being in the house," Pat told me. "I had one at least once a week, and they almost always stayed with me."

In one common dream, she would be walking down the stairs toward the front door. She'd stop halfway down, startled by something she couldn't identify. In another, she would be standing in the living room, gazing out the picture window at children playing in the front yard, a television babbling in the background. In still another sequence Pat described, she was in the front yard looking toward the house. It was because of this last sequence that Pat said she recognized the house when she came upon it.

What I found most interesting was that, in the dreams, the house was Pat's. She was adamant about that, and she was very sure that the children she saw from the front window — two boys and a girl — were hers. As a matter of fact, Pat told me that when she first saw this house from the road that fall day, the question "Why aren't there toys in the yard?" flashed through her mind for an instant.

Pat struck me as imaginative and somewhat superstitious but not abnormal. She came across as very sincere. With her permission, I called my old friend and teacher Fr. John Kiley, a Roman Catholic priest and psychologist, who arranged a thorough psychiatric evaluation at the Institute of Living in Hartford, today a facility of Hartford Hospital's mental-health program.

In the meantime, I was determined to track down the couple in Maine who had been struck with abject horror at Patricia DeVito's very presence. Fortunately, Jan had caught a name on the mailbox: Kalinowski. The town they were driving through at the time, she said, was York.

In an uncanny stroke of luck, my mother's family had owned a vacation home at nearby York Beach for nearly a century, and I had vacationed in the area all my life. I knew a few people in town. Through these handy contacts, I managed to get an address and phone number (which was unlisted) for the only Kalinowskis in the vicinity.

I thought it best to introduce the subject, and myself, by letter rather than by telephone. I wrote on October 22, and I included every professional reference I could think of so the couple would realize I wasn't some kind of nut. Frankly, I didn't expect an answer before the holidays were over, if at all. To my amazement and delight, I answered the telephone only four days later to find a deeply shaken Peter Kalinowski at the other end.

"This is very difficult for us, but we have to talk to somebody who won't think we're crazy," Peter told me. The man sounded like a complete wreck. Not knowing who I was, of course, he evidently had called every one of the clergy, teachers and doctors I'd given as references.

Footsteps in the Attic

"They tell me you're not a publicity hound," he went on. "We're not going to talk to you unless you guarantee in writing that you'll keep what we tell you confidential."

While I thought this was a little "over the wall," I bit my tongue and agreed. Writing this nearly twenty-three years later, however, I think the "statute of limitations" is up on that particular promise.

So the day after Hallowe'en found me turning into the driveway of the house in question, a plain, two-story, '60s-era home on a back road a few miles from the quaint village of York Harbor. The first thing I noticed was a "For Sale" sign on the front lawn.

Peter Kalinowski opened the door before I'd even stepped out of the car.

At the door where Pat DeVito had caused such terror, I found a childless couple in early middle age. They were two very frightened people. Inside, Ann Kalinowski offered me some coffee, which I declined (I never touch the stuff). Her hands shook. She looked like she could have used some Scotch.

"I really checked you out," were the first words out of Peter's mouth. "We don't want anybody hearing about this, but we just want some answers. We've barely slept since this happened!"

As in so many other cases, the Kalinowskis' first concern was whether they were "going crazy."

As I say in the introduction to this book, there are all sorts of explanations for hearing and seeing things, and most of them are not paranormal: neural conditions such as temporal-lobe epilepsy (something many doctors immediately look for when a patient reports paranormal experiences), psychiatric conditions such as schizophrenia, or simply optical illusions.

But the story I heard from this couple made the hair stand up on the back of even *my* neck. In absolute fascination, I listened to Peter and Ann describe the numerous occasions they had seen a transparent figure they adamantly claimed was "the girl at the door" in exactly the same positions Pat DeVito described in her dreams: walking half way down the stairs, looking out the living-room window and even standing in the front yard looking at the house.

Sometimes they'd witness these apparitions individually, sometimes together. "Pat" would make her appearances at all hours of the day and night, they said. So terrified had Peter and Ann become that, in the weeks before DeVito and company had arrived at their door, they had taken to sticking close to each other while at home.

Interestingly, the Kalinowskis were convinced that the stairway apparition "seemed to see them." But it would look not so much *at* them as *through* them, they said. I immediately recalled Pat's description of her dreams: walking halfway down the stairs and being startled by something she couldn't identify. She reported seeing no people. And, yes: Just as Pat's dreams about the house had stopped when she finally encountered the place, so had the apparitions, according to the Kalinowskis.

In the course of long interviews with the couple, first individually and then together, I saw no signs that they were anything but very sincere and very frightened.

Meanwhile, Pat was undergoing the Minnesota Multiphasic Personality Inventory® test, a modern version of which is still used as a first step in evaluating people's psychopathology. It revealed nothing especially abnormal about her. She was highly imaginative, with a tendency to gloss over problems, but that was about it.

Pat never met the Kalinowskis again, but I kept in touch with her and them throughout 1979. In that time, neither the couple nor the girl ever reported another significant paranormal experience. "The Haunter," as I call it, remains one of the most fascinating and mystifying cases I

Footsteps in the Attic

have ever dealt with.

Back in the parapsychological stone age of the 1970s, my equipment consisted of a few cameras, some recording gear, a notebook and a pen. I had no gauss meter (to measure electromagnetic fields), no bevy of experts and consultants, and I had never heard of the multiple-worlds interpretation of quantum physics. So I fell back on research that my friend, the late D. Scott Rogo, had been conducting on out-of-the-body experiences (OBEs).

In his California research in the 1970s and early 1980s with his colleague, parapsychologist Keith Harary, Scott cited several cases in which someone reported "astral projecting" and someone else reported seeing that person's "astral body" at the place to which they "projected."

I considered the Kalinowski case just a variation on this phenomenon. But I was confused by one thing: Patricia's insistence that there were children at the house and that they belonged to her. I scratched my head for awhile, realized that Scott had noted several cases in which "astral projectors" had ended up in what seemed like quite different worlds, and chalked up Pat's children issue to something like that.

Little did I realize how correct I probably was! Looking back on it from the perspective of quantum reality and the multiverse, I believe that what the Kalinowskis and Pat DeVito went through was *a mutual experience of the same parallel universes.*

According to researchers like Scott, people who experience OBEs often do so while asleep, as in Pat's dreams. But where did Pat project *to?* Just to that house in York Harbor, Maine?

I don't think so.

I'm convinced that Pat didn't so much "project her consciousness," as many OBE researchers believe, as connect with that facet of her consciousness that already carried on daily life in the Maine house in a parallel world in which it was her house and those were her children. If I'm right, then how many other ghosts are just shadows of people carrying on their lives somewhere else, wondering about those weird and vivid dreams that they can't get out of their minds? And how impossibly rare are those cases in which the "projector" and the percipient actually encounter one another in the same day-to-day reality?

In over thirty years of research, this is the only one I've ever dealt with first-hand. How many more have happened that we know nothing about?

Footsteps in the Attic

The Phantom House

After enduring the Bridgeport poltergeist outbreak of November 1974 (see *Faces at the Window*, New River Press, 1998), I thought I had seen everything. But the following summer brought one of the oddest cases I had encountered up to that point: a house that apparently was itself a ghost.

I was visiting friends in rural Vermont that July, not far from the village of Enosburg Falls. Ironically, the place is named after my great-great-great-great granduncle, Roger Enos, a Revolutionary War general once accused of treason by, of all people, Benedict Arnold!

One clear evening, while we lounged on the porch enjoying the crickets, a few whippoorwills, and some quiet conversation, a bright red pickup truck bounced into the driveway in a cloud of dust. The occupants turned out to be Clement Ridley and Bud Harper, two surveyors from "downcountry" who had driven up to meet me. After some talk about my recent cases, especially Bridgeport, one of my friends looked at Ridley.

"Well, are you going to tell him?"

"He'll think we're crazy – or drunk," Ridley quipped with a long pull on his bottle of beer.

"I've heard everything at least twice," I reassured him. In fact, I'd never heard anything quite like what he was going to tell me.

The previous summer, it seems, Ridley and Harper were getting ready to survey boundaries for a farmer in the Town of Johnson, about twenty miles south of where we sat.

"I was walking the bounds with my partner, and we had the (U.S. Geological Survey) map of the area. We'd just come out of the woods into a field and were walking a little downhill. It was early afternoon, and we sat down on the ground to look at the map and think about the survey we were going to start," Ridley recalled.

"You know, these USGS maps have all the main buildings and houses on them that were there when they made the map. Now there was a good-sized old farmhouse just across this field, about a quarter-mile away where there was an old dirt road that marked the property boundary. And the house wasn't on the map."

Shaking their heads at government inefficiency, the two men completed their walk down to the road, which was rutted and little used.

"We were in the road about sixty feet from the house now, and it was pretty dilapidated. Old as hell and surrounded by a stone wall. The house didn't look as if it had ever been painted," Harper chimed in. "But you could tell somebody lived there. There was smoke coming out of the chimney, even though it was a warm day, and there were clothes on the line."

That's when they saw the man, according to Ridley.

"He came around a corner of the house with an axe over his shoulder. Slim guy with a broad-brimmed hat and a big beard. Couldn't really tell how old he was."

The two men noted that the "whole scene was strange." No cars or trucks in the yard, no electrical wires overhead, no other signs of life.

"I was curious where the guy's property lines were, so I called to him. He didn't seem to hear me. Just kept going toward the front, then stooped to look at something on the ground," Harper said.

Ridley shouted to the man, then started to walk toward the stone wall.

"The guy just stood up and looked around, kind of confused. But he still didn't seem to see us. It was really weird. We figured the guy might be a little deaf, but he must have been blind, too!" Ridley declared.

The two surveyors started to feel uncomfortable.

"There are still some pretty strange people in these hills,

and the guy had an axe. We figured that retreat 'was the better part of valor,'" he added.

A few days later, the surveying job began.

"When we got back to that field and that road, we were shocked to see that the damn house wasn't even there! There was no sign of it!" Ridley said. "We didn't make a mistake about where we were – maps don't lie!"

Ridley was at the Johnson Town Hall a few days later and, still flummoxed, made some inquiries. According to town records, there had been an old house on that road, but it had burned down in 1910!

The day after our conversation on the porch, Ridley and Harper took me to the site. Several turns off the main road, we came to a little lane that meandered toward the nearby mountains. It was so rutted and muddy that we had to plow along with four-wheel drive.

"There it is – or was," Ridley muttered, pointing out the window toward the road's wooded border on the left.

The men were quiet as we got out of the truck and approached what I could see were the remains of a stone wall and an almost-vanished foundation. My companions still seemed spooked. Creeping phlox and dwarf conifers, which love rocky ground and are common at abandoned homesites in New England, were abundant. I kicked about the place but found nothing unusual. I did notice that a few of the old foundation stones were blackened as if by fire.

We left just as mystified as we had come. I had no reason to doubt the two men who had told me the story, but I did doubt that I had even begun to fathom the true depths of the paranormal.

Today, of course, I know that my acquaintances had been eye-to-eye with an extradimensional event – a space-time displacement – and I've since collected many such cases. But back in 1975, I was learning that there is far more to ghostly phenomena than just ghosts.

Footsteps in the Attic

Face to Face with a Druid

This book is supposed to be about the paranormal in *New* England, but it's worth stretching a point to include two amazing cases I encountered in old England, ones that continue to illustrate the reality of "ghosts from elsewhen."

As long as I've been a ghost hunter, it's still a shock when paranormal sights and sounds happen suddenly, as they usually do. I'm more of a ghost "feeler": I'm very good at sensing their presence but I rarely see them. What happened to me in the West Country of England was a notable exception.

In 1988 and 1989, I made two busy but delightful trips to the mother country. I was there primarily to research Britain's "big cat" phenomena, particularly the splendidly named "Black Beast of Exmoor" in the northern part of the County of Devon, in southwest England. My "beast" researches are another story entirely, but I have no wish to torture the reader. So, in brief: Since the early 1980s, farmers in several parts of Britain have reported livestock killed by a mysterious, black, cougar-like creature. Cougars or mountain lions aren't native to Britain, therefore the mystery. The instances I was researching centered in and around Exmoor and Dartmoor, two magnificent national parks and wilderness areas that are like something out of a Thomas Hardy novel. As a matter of fact, Sir Arthur Conan Doyle set the Sherlock Holmes thriller *The Hound of the Baskervilles* on Dartmoor. Magnificently bleak, it's an appropriate setting for mysterious creatures.

For me there was a personal connection with the area and its sweet-spirited people because mobs of my ancestors came from Devon and adjacent Somerset. But I must say that if I never see another sheep it will be too soon. I interviewed farmers and other witnesses, examined sheep kills and followed huge, feline footprints over roll-

Photo by Paul F. Eno

The patch of vegetation at the left center is the mysterious Wistman's Wood, one of the wonders of England's Dartmoor region.

ing moors and into mystifying woodlands where the last of the Druids once hid from Roman soldiers, who didn't take kindly to their annoying habit of human sacrifice.

You'll have to wait for another book to find out what happened with "the beast," but for the purposes of this one let's look at what I encountered on my way back to London for the trip home.

It was March 1989 and, enraptured by this austere and mystical country, I decided to take an afternoon and visit the three hundred sixty-five square-mile Dartmoor National Park. I ended up in the tiny hamlet of Two Bridges, in south Devon, and stopped for lunch at the quaint Two Bridges Hotel, on the banks of the little West Dart River.

The British love to walk, a healthy habit that almost makes up for their unhealthy diet, and the whole United Kingdom is laced with hiking trails — public footpaths, as they're called. So I asked one of the hotel staff if he could suggest a good walk. He said that a little more than a mile across the moor was a place called Wistman's Wood, one of the oldest forests in Britain and supposedly haunted. I later looked up the name "Wistman's" and found that its most common interpretation is "wizard's."

Anyway, haunted woods being "right up my alley," off I went! Crossing the road, I struck a footpath that took me past a lovely old farm and out onto the moor. Having spent the previous week running around north Devon's Exmoor National Park in pursuit of "the beast," I was falling in love with these unique expanses of open wilderness.

Photo by Paul F. Eno

Wistman's Wood

Despite the fact that they are only about forty miles apart, Exmoor and Dartmoor have quite different characteristics. But on both, distances can be misleading, and fogs and mists can come up seemingly out of nowhere. Here and there, the walker even comes upon ancient burial mounds (known as "barrows") or circles of prehistoric standing stones, where cameras sometimes won't work and compasses often go wrong. Exmoor's landscape is more hilly and rolling, with deep valleys here and there. On Dartmoor, hills topped with bizarre outcrops of rock, known as "tors," rise up both nearby and on the horizon, lending a further aura of the otherworldly.

Telltale monuments to human prehistory are everywhere, and one of the most striking of these came into view as I crested a little rise above the farm at Two

Bridges. From where I stood, it looked almost like a patch of tall and ragged brown grass on the eastern slope of the moor just above the river. But as I approached, I could see that it was indeed a small woodland of only a few acres, such as I'd never seen before. The trees — ancient, gnarled and stunted — are miniature oaks, battered by centuries of unrelenting winds and bitter winters. The tallest tree I saw was only about twelve feet high. Together they stand like a tangled knot of ghosts on the slopes of Longaford Tor, their roots twining among hundreds of huge granite boulders, apparently dropped there by glaciers during the last Ice Age.

In almost preposterous contrast, a glance across the West Dart River to the opposite hillside revealed a fence line and signs warning of a military training area with occasional live-fire exercises.

In my fascination with Wistman's Wood, however, I admit that I ignored the signs posted by environmental authorities asking visitors to keep out of the actual woodland. There was an aura of ominous anticipation about the place, as though I were stepping through a portal into an alien time. It wasn't an unfamiliar feeling: That electrical tingle had hit me many times before in hundreds of haunted places. The tension seemed heightened by the utter silence of everything but the thin March wind.

I stepped inside, and out of the twentieth century. As I moved about among the twisted roots and strewn boulders, I soon saw that Wistman's Wood actually is two separate groves with an odd little swath running down the middle. I later learned that this swath traces the subsurface path of a large vein of quartz. From a geomagnetic standpoint, this is a clue to the presence of electrical fields that, in my opinion, could play games with space-time and give Wistman's Wood its haunted reputation.

I picked my way around the southern grove, touching

tree and rock, and enjoying the atmosphere of total timelessness. There were no birds, no insects, no animals: only the trees, oddly unmoved by a wind that seemed far away. I was surprised, out of the corner of my eye, to catch a movement to my right. As I turned my head, there was just an instant of blackness — like that sliver of blank time in a slide show between one image and another — and a heightened electrical tingle on my skin. In another instant, my consciousness focused again.

About thirty feet away, to the north, between me and one of the larger trees, was a figure. More specifically, there was *half* a figure. I could see nothing from the waist down, but above that was a man with his right side toward me. Dressed in what appeared to be a combination of brownish furs and a black cloak, with a round fur cap, he was staring intently eastward.

In another instant, he turned with a jerky movement and looked toward me. I don't say "at" me because I was certain that he couldn't see me. A second later, I suddenly experienced that sliver of blackness again and was quite alone once more.

The whole episode lasted about eight seconds, not bad as paranormal experiences go. I stood silent for awhile, savoring what to me was a rare and precious encounter. Depending on their own beliefs and backgrounds, friends later told me that I had a temporal-lobe experience, saw a classic ghost or simply was punch drunk from chasing fictitious monsters all over the moors for a week.

The attentive reader won't be surprised when I say that I'm partial to the idea that I had a classic space-time experience: a glimpse around the corner of that self-created wall we know as time, aided by the strange electromagnetic fields at Wistman's Wood. Barring that, the temporal-lobe experience comes in a strong second. But isn't it possible that one goes hand in hand with the other? I ask again, as I did in the introduction to the book: Do

Footsteps in the Attic

neural conditions such as temporal-lobe epilepsy (which there is no medical evidence that I have, by the way) create paranormal experiences within the mind, as is generally believed, or do they open paths for the mind into other times and places? I think the latter possibility deserves serious study rather than shaken heads.

In any case, I believe that I may well have encountered someone from "elsewhen" in that truly magical place. I call it a precious experience because, for one thing, I am a lover of history. I love it because history is people: People who may live in different worlds but who are one with us in human joys and sorrows.

Who was this man I saw staring so intently eastward? A few over-stimulated neurons firing in my brain or a fellow human from the distant past – or future? Was he one of the legendary Druids? An escaped prisoner from a far century? A cold hunter out of some dim decade, longing for home? One of my own ancestors? I doubt if I'll ever truly know.

Staring Across the Centuries

As my 1989 English trip drew to a close and I still puzzled over my strange Druid "ghost," I decided to make an overnight stop in the County of Kent — on the other side of the country from Devon — to see an old military buddy, Steve Hitchins. Steve was a Canadian-born teacher then living in Ramsgate on the so-called Isle of Thanet.

On a chilly March evening Steve and I found ourselves in The Red Lion, a wondrous old pub reputedly in continuous operation since the 1600s. Before long, three local men Steve knew breezed through the quaint doorway. We all joined up and, finding out that I was a Yank, they started chattering about American football and country music. Finding to their shock that I could have cared less about either, Steve redeemed me by announcing that I was a paranormal researcher and author. Well, that did it. The three switched to "full automatic" and started pelting me with tales of every local ghost they could think of, including several that reportedly made life interesting at The Red Lion.

"Wait a moment!" one lad suddenly chirped. "Tell him about Cleve Court!"

As it turned out, one of them, whose name was George, claimed to be the grandnephew of one Edward G. Moon, a local doctor who had an astonishing experience at Cleve Court, a large country house just north of the nearby village of Minster.

"He (the late doctor), never liked to talk about it," George declared. "You had to prod him."

Once prodded, though, Dr. Moon slowly would recall the day in 1934 when he had come home from Cleve Court "white as a sheet," scaring the daylights out of his good wife. At the time, the doctor was caring for Cleve Court's famous resident, the elderly Sir Edward Henry

Carson, Lord Carson of Duncairn, a well known lawyer and former member of Parliament who had been a big cheese in unionist politics in Northern Ireland. As a matter of fact, he's considered the "Father of Northern Ireland," which some Irish friends of mine consider a dubious distinction.

Copyright Edward Carson

Sir Edward Carson

Sir Edward had terminal lung disease, and Dr. Moon visited him nearly every day. As George told it, his granduncle emerged from Cleve Court one afternoon after checking on Sir Edward — and stepped straight into another time. As he left the house and stood on the front steps, Dr. Moon was looking down, mulling the not-so-great state of his patient. Then he glanced up.

"The first thing he saw was that his car was gone," George said. "Cleve Court even then had a horseshoe-shaped driveway out to the road, and that was gone, too, along with the hedge. And the road wasn't the road.... It was just a muddy track through a field!"

Then Dr. Moon spotted "the man," who already had seen him.

"He told me the man was about a hundred feet away and was dressed in eighteenth or nineteenth century riding clothes, and he had a riding crop that he kept hitting against his leg. He was staring at my uncle and finally stopped where he was," George recalled.

The doctor, whom George insisted was a man of rigid scientific attitudes, was numb with fear and confusion. Dr. Moon rubbed his eyes and looked again, only to see that his car, and 1934, were back where he had left them!

Footsteps in the Attic

According to George, the doctor never quite got over the experience, which shook him up from head to toe. I daresay we could say the same for the poor sap from "elsewhen," who presumably saw an oddly-dressed figure either on the steps of the house or, worse, suspended in midair.

Sir Edward didn't do so well either: He died the following year.

Of course, the whole thing could have been a psychiatric or neural episode, but George claimed that the doctor had never reported an experience like it and never did so again.

I'm always skeptical about second-hand stories, even from the percipient's relatives, and I wasn't in Kent long enough to find out more about the story, though I have seen several versions of it reported in a few obscure sources since then. I've researched many of these stories and have found them to be variations of urban legends or just outright frauds. Others, in my opinion, are quite genuine. I'm also skeptical if only one person experiences the event. But I'm not so pig-headed as to think this in itself means the experience isn't real.

Aside from the fact that Dr. Moon supposedly was a no-nonsense sort of guy, I'm apt to accept George's story for two reasons. For one thing, the annals of the paranormal are filled with tales of ghostly happenings (many experienced by several people at once) that I believe are "legit" and that to me are dead ringers for time displacements such as Dr. Moon experienced.

For another, Cleve Court has a very telltale paranormal history. I did manage to do a little research on the place before catching the plane for Boston. As a matter of fact, Steve took me to the house the day after that evening in the pub.

A lovely, very old home set back from the road, Cleve Court is listed in the National Trust (Britain's equivalent

Footsteps in the Attic

of the National Register of Historic Places). It was a private dwelling, so we didn't go inside. The horseshoe driveway was still there, as was the hedge. But it was hardly the quietest place on Earth: Kent International Airport, which shared the site with RAF Manston, a Royal Air Force base dating back to World War II, was across the road, just to the southeast. In fact, a U.S. Air Force plane blew a tire on takeoff one day in 1956 and ended up in the wall of the house!

The oldest part of Cleve Court dates to at least 1500, and subsequent occupants added to the place. Before the Carsons, who moved there in 1920, another famous resident was the Hungarian-born British author Baroness Emmuska Orczy, who wrote the *The Scarlet Pimpernel*, along with other plays and novels, and was a big name in the 1920s.

According to local stories, one of the early owners had kept his wife locked in the house while he carried on with other women. This wife supposedly had longed for a son or a daughter, but had died childless. Of course, this is a classic campfire ghost story. I can just taste the marshmallows! But true or not, it apparently gave the Carsons a run for their money at Cleve Court. As I heard it, Lady Carson started noticing funny goings-on as soon as somebody told her this story. She was alarmed when youthful guests wanted to know who the "grey lady" was who kept walking in and out of their rooms. Guests would see this apparition standing over the beds of their sleeping children, a typical phenomenon in many houses I've investigated.

The long-widowed Lady Carson supposedly never saw the ghost until 1949. That happened very early one morning when her cocker spaniel had to answer a collect call from Mother Nature. When Lady Carson and the dog started back upstairs, the pair froze in their tracks: Coming down the stairs toward them — from the direction of

Lady Carson's bedroom, if you don't mind — was the famous "Grey Lady," complete with flowing gown.

As the story appeared in several contemporary newspaper articles, the Grey Lady got to the landing halfway down the stairs, then pivoted through a door that led into a part of the house built in the Elizabethan era. Needless to say, both Lady Carson and doggie were scared stiff, and made a hasty retreat downstairs.

After the papers got hold of the story, apparently from a neighbor Lady Carson had confided in, a former servant wrote to the shaken widow. The ex-maid recounted her own experience, while she was working at seven one morning in the Elizabethan part of the house. She had heard footsteps in the hallway, she said. When she looked, she claimed that a woman in old-fashioned clothes looked at her, made a motion that the maid should stay put, then vanished.

According to the maid, other staff members had scoffed at the story. As the tale was told to me, Lady Carson later learned that earlier occupants and staff had heard footsteps in the same hallway as far back as she could find.

These sorts of reports, actually quite common, always make me think back to "the haunter" in York Harbor, Maine. I believe that, along with Dr. Moon's experience, what happened to Lady Carson, the maid and, apparently, numerous other people at Cleve Court, were space-time displacements.

Even the apparent interaction between the phantom lady and the maid, with the former seeming to attempt communication, doesn't steer me away from that conclusion. Just as Patricia DeVito, in her dream of walking down the stairs in Maine, stopped after seeming to notice something to her left, the phantom lady, aware only of her own time and place, could easily have been motioning to one of her own servants standing in the same place.

Footsteps in the Attic

As I say elsewhere, I don't believe that ghosts like this are spirits of the dead forced to relive traumatic events for all and sundry to see. I believe they are people in their own time and place who connect with others, and have their own paranormal experience, because the people and energies are just right at that moment and place.

I haven't had a chance to research this yet, but I'll bet my right eyebrow that there are electromagnetic fields in the Manston area that contribute to these space-time displacements. I'll wager that I'd get funny readings on my gauss meter for no apparent reason and that, at certain times and places there, my compass would be off.

I hope to get back to Cleve Court sometime to gather more data along these lines. If I'm lucky, I may even meet the Grey Lady or that flustered guy with the riding crop!

The Lady in the Attic

If Woonsocket, Rhode Island, the old New England mill town where I live, is any example, paranormal phenomena are pervasive. I turn up now and again in the state and local media, especially when they drag me out at Hallowe'en, so people in northern Rhode Island tend to know who I am. I frequently get calls from local folks who want help with ghosts. Often enough it turns out to be nothing, but once in a while I encounter something, or someone, quite interesting. This was the case one day in late 2000 when some friends from the other side of town suddenly chimed in: "You know, we have a ghost!"

It was about two years since Red and Bernice Hamilton had moved into the beautiful, wood-and-brick house in Woonsocket's high-class North End.

"Well," said Red, an easy-going Ohio native, settling into a chair by the fireplace. "Many a morning I've come down those stairs and it looks as though somebody has just got up and walked away from that rocking chair, 'cause it's still rocking."

"Then there's that door at the bottom of the attic stairs. It just won't stay closed," Bernice chimed in.

Their son Harold had his own story.

"I was leaving for work about five o'clock one morning. I happened to glance up toward the attic window, and there was this blue light inside! I felt like somebody was looking at me!" he recalled.

Nothing especially alarming here, and nothing that couldn't be explained in some other way. Still, I was intrigued. For once, I knew the people telling these stories, and they weren't likely to be imagining or exaggerating. At the same time, I had little fear for them: The Hamiltons are among the most positive people I know. Their family is full of love, humor, faith, confidence and general good feeling. They weren't about to become a hot lunch for

Footsteps in the Attic

any parasitical entity, nor were they likely to "connect" in any negative way with some other part of the multiverse.

Checking things out a few days later, I got some elevated readings on my gauss meter in the attic area, where there really shouldn't have been a fluctuating field of one hundred to four hundred gauss, so I lined up a visit by some of my "gang." A few Saturdays later, we trooped in. On hand were my sidekick and "heir apparent" Shane Sirois; soil engineer Joe Frisella, and University of Rhode Island electrical-engineering professor Everett Crisman.

Red and Harold had been doing some remodeling in the attic and reported feeling a presence on several occasions.

"Didn't seem mad or hostile, more like curious," Red commented.

When our group arrived, nobody was home but Harold, so the five of us headed for the attic and settled in. Shane was in charge of photography because he has better equipment than I have. He also feels entities the same way I do.

As we stood near the doorway to the stairs, Shane and I simultaneously felt it arriving, just as though it were coming out of the roof above the stairway, or from a room that wasn't there – at least not in our part of space-time. There was that tingling electrical energy and that unmistakable feeling of presence – a strong female presence, like an old woman. Harold, Joe and Everett all felt what they described as "a breeze." Shane and I felt as though we were being "checked out."

Shane had started snapping digital photos, and the great thing about that is that you can see you've got right away. Sure enough, on one of the shots were two orbs, one of which was large and blue. Later computer enlargement showed what clearly seemed to be the face of an old woman within one orb. After a short time, Shane and I felt the presence leave the way it had come.

As I write this nearly two years later, this female presence continues to manifest in the Hamilton house now and then. While this remains mild and "curious," not a bother to the Hamiltons, I've kept an eye on this case. Lately, I've been intrigued to learn that their next-door neighbor has been experiencing similar phenomena all along. I'm not surprised at all to see this evidence that the land under the whole area is "energized" with the right sort of electromagnetic fields to pave the way for the paranormal. I plan to expand the investigation to include a wider area, with more involved soil studies and electromagnetic-field measurements.

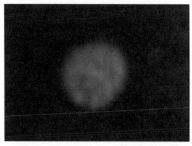

Photo by Shane Sirois

The lady in the attic?

It appears to me that part or all of the neighborhood may be in close parallel with another, quite similar, reality in space-time; perhaps more than one.

So what about our "lady in the attic"?

Well, if this situation is what it appears to be – an old woman who lives in a close parallel universe — I believe the Hamiltons have little to worry about. Whenever or wherever she may be, she appears to be psychically sensitive, checking out feelings of presences and sounds in her home just as the Hamiltons do in theirs. As she goes about her daily life, she's aware of them as they are of her.

Among the army of "ghosts from elsewhen" I have encountered over the years, there are many like the Hamiltons' "tenant": curious, non-threatening people from other places and times whom the vagaries of quantum reality have placed side by side with us.

Footsteps in the Attic

Nevertheless, I never let lapse that healthy dose of suspicion. My concern isn't for positive people like the Hamiltons. It's for whomever lives in the house after they do. If they're the wrong sort – negative people or occult practitioners – they could connect with negative entities through the same energy "windows" in space-time that allow the limited contact between us and "the lady."

Only space-time will tell.

Footsteps in the Attic

2

TORTURED SOULS

Footsteps in the Attic

I started out in the early 1970s working with ghost hunters who were head-over-heels sold on the Victorian séance-room theory: Ghosts are spirits of the dead caught between Earth and the "spirit world." They're lost souls who don't know they're dead and haven't "passed over correctly," whatever that means. Most amateur researchers today still buy into the same point of view. Those who don't often are psychologists or parapsychologists who miss the boat on quantum mechanics, straining and sweating to make phenomena they record fit an antiquated, materialist scientific model, which just isn't going to happen.

Well, there's a good reason ghosts don't know they're dead. They aren't. My conviction is that they're alive – body and all – in any number of parallel universes, just as we are. One of the more common reasons for these manifestations across the multiverse is what I call the "tortured soul": Someone in pain or personal upheaval who is so highly charged about it that the electromagnetic ripples roll back and forth across space-time. I'm convinced that this is the prime cause for the classic haunting.

In the 1995 film *Casper*, Bill Pullman plays a shrink dedicated to counseling ghosts, and the media chuckle over "the psychiatrist to the dead." Well, don't look now, but the man was onto something. It works!

While tortured souls actually are "ghosts from elsewhen," they get their own chapter because I have a soft spot for them and because they need a little "TLC."

The Crying Ghost

The Queridos heard nothing odd for the first four years they lived in the trim, 1950s-era house in Auburn, Massachusetts, just outside Worcester.

Then it began.

In the quiet of the night, even as the family's antique clock ticked reassuringly on the living-room mantle, the sobbing would start. Little Lori heard it first and, finally, her skeptical parents, Ann and John.

"I thought I was dreaming, but I was wide awake and it kept going. The crying, I mean," Ann Querido explained in a phone call to me in January 1991. "It's soft. It even fades in and out sometimes. But we've all heard it. And now I'm *really* scared because of what I saw in Lori's room!"

That's where I stopped her. In the early '90s, it already was my policy to go and see for myself before hearing the whole story or making any judgments.

I pulled up outside the Querido home on the morning of February 7, a sunny Thursday. Inside the five-room, Cape Cod-style house I found a worried-looking woman and a husky, curly-haired man, both in their early thirties. Both had taken the day off from work to meet me. Lori, the couple's five-year old daughter, was at morning kindergarten.

Touring the house and the yard with the couple in tow, I felt that the bathroom, the child's bedroom, part of the backyard, and the basement were indeed "charged." At the same time, I felt that "it" was moving. As a matter of fact, in the course of two hours in this house, I repeatedly followed this electrical field from the bathroom, down the hall to the child's room, out into the yard, then down to the basement, where it would vanish. All the while, I snapped away with my trusty 35-mm camera, but at the time I had no gauss meter or much else. For much of my career, ghost hunting has been very much a "seat-of-the-pants" operation!

One of the most striking impressions was an overwhelming feeling of sadness, even depression. Not evil, not hostility, not lifelessness, just sadness. To me, this already had become a familiar signature: a suffering human sending ripples through space-time.

At the same time, I noted how crowded this semi-urban neighborhood was. The Queridos' house and lot were small. There were many homes, both single-family and multi-family, nearby, and there was a good deal of car and truck traffic. Plenty of sources for a sound like crying.

When we finally sat down at the kitchen table that morning and I began my long list of standard questions, I quickly formed the impression that John and Ann were exactly what they appeared to be: an honest, blue-collar couple, faithful Roman Catholics who weren't playing with Ouija boards, séances or any of the other psychic dynamite that can blow open holes in space-time and attract big trouble. From what I could see, the Queridos' personal and family problems weren't explosive either.

Less chance for a parasitical entity with these folks around, I thought.

Then I listened to their story.

It was June 1986 when the Queridos moved in, truly a day of fulfillment and pride for them. John and Ann had worked and saved for years, and it was their first house. It also would be their first experience with a ghost.

In the wee hours of a Sunday morning in November 1990, little Lori had climbed out of bed and tramped sleepily into her parents' bedroom.

"Mommy!" she said, shaking Ann, "Somebody's crying."

"What's the matter, honey?" Ann asked groggily, thinking the child was talking about herself.

"I don't know. Somebody's crying. Come on!" the child replied, now tugging at Ann's sleeve.

Ann glanced at the clock as Lori pulled her out of bed: 1:15 a.m. The child led her mother down the short hallway and into her own room. The only sound was the ticking of the old living-room clock and John's heavy breathing back in the master bedroom.

"Lori, there's nothing. Go back to bed," Ann commanded.

It struck me at once that Lori obeyed without complaint. She didn't seem particularly afraid, according to Ann, which meant that perhaps we were dealing with something non-threatening. Children can relate to crying. They do it and see it often. Perhaps all this wasn't paranormal at all. All sorts of things, from cats to major appliances, can make sounds like crying. But I couldn't forget the striking impressions I'd picked up earlier. This could very well be a "ghost from elsewhen."

Why the four-year wait for phenomena to begin? I find that it often takes people two to four years in a new home to "connect" electromagnetically with whatever is there. Just as a relationship between two people takes time to develop, so does a relationship between people and their environment. I believe it's that simple.

The next night at 1:30 a.m., Lori was back at Ann and John's bedside. Ann once again heard nothing. And the child was back the night after that. By this time, mom was losing patience.

"This is the last time, Lori!" Ann growled as she heaved out of bed once more.

Then she froze.

"You see, mommy?"

Ann didn't see. She heard. It was indeed a muffled but pathetic sound very much like sobbing. It faded "back and forth," as she later described it to me. John was a heavy sleeper, and it took some doing for Ann to shake

Footsteps in the Attic

him awake. When she finally did, he heard it too.

"I tried to figure out where it was coming from," John told me. "But I just couldn't get around the idea that it was someplace in the house."

Lori crawled into bed with her parents and soon was fast asleep. The sounds died away in about another ten minutes, but John and Ann lay awake for the rest of the night.

The next morning, a fine Saturday with the sun glinting off an inch of new, late-spring snow, John and Ann sat at the kitchen table rationalizing, as most people do after a paranormal experience.

"We told ourselves that it had to be coming from next door someplace, or maybe outside."

That night, with Lori in bed with them again, the sobbing started. Ann heard it first and woke John. It kept going for a few nights, then stopped.

The crying was one thing, I thought, but I was just as alarmed as Ann was over the apparition.

"There hadn't been any crying for a couple of nights, then I just woke up one night and it was like things were *too* quiet. I can't explain it!" she told me.

Uneasy, Ann climbed out of bed and glided down the darkened hallway to Lori's room. When she stepped through the doorway, every muscle froze and every hair on the back of her neck stood up. Ann shook as she described the scene.

"It was a ghost! I actually saw a ghost! There was some light from the street and this shimmery thing with like robes and a face – I saw the face clear as day. She was looking at Lori in the bed! That face broke my heart. It was a woman – a sad, sad woman! My God, I was petrified!"

Then Ann's mother instinct got the better of her terror.

"I started to get mad. What was this thing going to do to my baby?"

Footsteps in the Attic

Forcing her legs to move, Ann stepped forward. At once, without looking at Ann, the "thing" vanished. Ann called me the next day.

I pressed her with generic questions, and she finally described another common trait of the paranormal experience, one that many people ignore – that half-second blackout, almost like a slide changing in a projector, and a sudden awareness of the paranormal event. It's happened to me often, and I believe it's the slip of a "veil," if I may use that hackneyed term, between one part of space-time and another.

There indeed can be brief and very limited interaction with ghosts during space-time displacements, but any interaction makes me suspicious because of the possibility for parasitical entities. Those miserable critters can come across as crying ghosts, jolly old gents or just about anything else – until they start getting nasty. On the other hand, I've found that looking into cribs and children's beds seems to be a favorite pastime of "tortured souls." I don't believe that they see what we see. They're in their own universes, after all, and I have every reason to believe that they see things as they would in their niche in the multiverse. Most likely, they get feelings of being watched by us just as we do by them. They walk over and check out noises and feelings just as we do.

Nevertheless, I advised the Queridos to have Lori sleep in their room until we'd gotten to the bottom of this. The pictures I'd taken on that first visit seemed perfectly normal.

I was forming tentative conclusions, not just because of the story I'd heard and the impressions of sadness I was getting, but based on experience. The repetitive path the ghost took through the house, into the yard and down to the basement was a pattern I'd seen before. I didn't tell the Queridos this – yet – but it was my bet there had been a suicide here, not in this house but in another on the same spot in a different part of space-time.

How much suffering must someone endure before they begin fearing life more than death? Suicide. It has been at the root of a number of my cases, and it probably produces more "tortured souls" than any other experience that sends waves of pain echoing out over space-time. The impressions I get in such places can be heart-wrenching. I myself often feel like crying.

I would have bet my breakfast that a woman in a house on this spot somewhere in space-time had lost a child and taken her own life in despair – or would in the "future." On the off chance that such a suicide had taken place in our historical time and could be pinned down, I set one of my crew, Mitch Norbock, at the time a student at Worcester's Clark University, to some local historical research. He didn't find any suicides traceable to the Queridos' address. But he did find that the houses in that part of Auburn had replaced an older, working-class neighborhood torn down in the 1950s.

Meanwhile, I was determined to hear this spook for myself. I lined up the "crying" dates Ann and John recalled, and it seemed that it happened most often around the time of the full moon. No joke, and no superstition. The full moon affects the Earth's magnetic field – and therefore our electromagnetic environment and our own brain functions – just as it does the tides. "Ghosts from elsewhen" really do tend to be more apparent at times of the full moon because they're electrical, too.

I still was working as a night editor at the *Providence Journal*, so my day usually ran until 2:30 a.m. anyway. Late hours didn't faze me. I arrived in Auburn just before the chilly midnight of March 29. Very conveniently, it not only was the day before the full moon, it was a Friday, too, so the Queridos could wait up with me.

Lori was snoozing blissfully in her parents' bed, and Ann, John and I chatted quietly in the darkened living room. By 12:45, John had nodded off and was snoring contentedly. By 1, Ann's head was drooping. I was wide awake, so, with a thrill, I heard it first. Unmistakably, it was the sound of a woman sobbing, but it was difficult to pin down just where it was coming from.

The pain of it touched me deeply. This was no parasite! I got up very slowly, moving ever so quietly into the hallway. It seemed to be coming from Lori's room. I moved toward it and peered through the door. Was that a slight shimmer by the bed? I couldn't be sure!

All of a sudden it seemed to be coming from the bathroom. I got there, and it was back in the hallway! This had happened to me frequently in the past. I'd run toward a sound, only to have it pop up again somewhere nearby. Einstein, remember, theorized that space-time is literally curved.

I swung suddenly to look back toward the living room. My heart skipped a beat when I clearly saw a figure there. Just Ann! She and John both were awake, and both heard the sobbing, fading in and out as though from near to far. I had no doubt it was a distance that couldn't be measured in inches, feet or miles.

Back in the living room, I sat the couple down.

"Let's try something before it stops," I whispered. "Let's hold hands, calm down and quiet our minds as much as we can."

When I felt that my companions had done so, at least as much as they were going to, I spoke up.

"Peace, dear," I said to the darkness. "Peace."

The third time I said this, the sobbing suddenly stopped. I got the very sharp impression that whoever it was was vaguely aware of us, uncertain and afraid. I got more confident with what I was doing. I whispered to Ann and John.

"I don't think she can actually hear us. I think she's feeling us. Whatever you do, project love and compassion,"

Footsteps in the Attic

I advised.

I spoke toward our ghost again.

"You are not alone. You are loved. You are not alone!"

Not a peep. But the sense of sadness seemed a little less.

There was no more activity that night. When I left an excited but groggy Ann and John at about 2:30 a.m., I urged them to build up this feeling of compassion, love, solidarity and even humor in the house. I advised them to pray fervently and often for this poor woman, who-ever she was or would be.

I was wonderfully gratified only a few weeks later when I talked with Ann by phone. She was in tears, but they were the tears of someone who has been deeply moved.

"We did what you said. We prayed and we told her we loved her. My God, Paul! Everything started to feel so wonderful and, like, clean! There was never any more crying. But last night we all woke up at the same time, around midnight, and I swear the whole house smelled like flowers! It was the most beautiful thing I've ever felt!"

Then she let me in on the "grand finale."

"John and I came out of the bedroom and into the kitchen this morning. We were all happy. Then, right in the middle of the kitchen floor, we saw this big, beauti-ful lily! No idea where it could have come from. Just one cut lily, biggest one I ever saw!"

Of course, the flower could have gotten there in any number of ways, but the Queridos saw it as a parting "thank-you" gift from their uninvited guest.

Well, why not?

The Frustrated Teacher

Probably the only case I've ever had in which the people involved were more terrified of the publicity than they were of the ghost was at a large Massachusetts elementary school.

I don't dare tell you where it was, and if you have children you'll understand why. Every school has its ghost stories, ninety-five percent of them silly urban legends, in my opinion. All an authority figure, especially a teacher or parent, has to do is tell a campfire ghost story or make a jocular remark about "the ghost that scared the janitor" or "the kid who died at the end of the hallway." Rest assured that youngsters will repeat it and embellish it for generations. And if children actually see evidence that a story is true, or hear adults saying so, chaos and terror will ensue in the halls of learning.

This actually began to happen at the school in question in June 1993. I first heard about it when I picked up the phone to hear the school's principal. As you can imagine, I've had some pretty odd phone conversations, but this one took the giddy biscuit.

"Is this Paul Eno?"

"Yes, sir. What can I do for you?"

"Is this Paul Eno the...ah...ghost expert."

"As far as I know. What can I do for you?"

"I...ah...really can't begin to explain...."

And so on for another minute. The man was so embarrassed that I had to lead him to the subject. I thought I'd better scrap procedure this once and just hear the story outright, or this case would take years. When he finally came clean, here's what I got:

Classroom 305 had been strange as long as anyone could remember. The two janitors, who almost always arrived first in the morning and left last at day's end, experienced the most oddities there. When they could be cajoled into talking about it, which was seldom, they would mutter about voices and footsteps heard in the room. They hated to wax the floors because cleaning tools would disappear. And when they rearranged desks, they'd often turn around to find the desks back in their original positions. They didn't even like using the janitors' room next to Classroom 305.

Things didn't just happen off-hours, either.

Teachers never liked to use 305. As each year began, they'd badger the administration to palm it off on some unsuspecting new colleague. Before long, he or she would complain of missing books and papers, odd scrawls on the blackboard first thing in the morning and even furniture moved about when nobody was looking. Occasionally, there were feelings of an "angry" presence. There even were complaints that students were more rowdy in 305 than in any other classroom.

Then there were the apparitions. According to the principal, every three or four years, from time out of mind, someone would report seeing a "shimmery" female figure moving rapidly back and forth across the front of the room or along the windows. As far as he knew, there had never been any direct interaction with this entity, if entity it was.

"I'm not saying I believe all this," he told me. "But the stories are getting out of hand among the kids. I've even had a parent on the phone about it! This has to be nipped before the press gets hold of it! We heard you don't get the press involved."

Well, school officials had heard right, but so much for my policy of seeing for myself before hearing the works! Even after the man had blurted out the whole story, it wasn't that easy to start an investigation: The superintendent of schools and members of the School Committee wanted to interview me first! That was a little galling when I wasn't even getting paid for this.

Footsteps in the Attic

"No cameras," the woman, a School Committee member, declared hands-down as I sat across the table from four big shots that weekend. I had come all the way up to meet with them, and I'd just explained how I worked.

"But I need photographs to help me find out what's going on. I can't get rid of it if I don't know what it is!"

"No cameras!"

They even made me sign a paper stating that I wouldn't utter a whisper or jot down a letter about the case for five years, and even then I couldn't name the school or even the city. I felt as though I were dealing with the CIA. They seemed to like the rest of my approach and my theories, however. The superintendent remarked cheerily that I "didn't seem like a flake." He acted surprised.

At least they gave me dinner after this inquisition.

A few days later I appeared in the teacher's room at the school just after classes dismissed for the day. There I interviewed four faculty members and both janitors, who told me much the same things the principal had. The powers that were wouldn't let me interview any students, however.

The superintendent, who hovered annoyingly about during the whole procedure, seemed as nervous as a cat in a room full of rocking chairs. The principal, on the other hand, was starting to get comfortable with all this. He breezed in just as I finished the last interview. By late that day, in fact, he'd apparently appointed himself my assistant. I much prefer working alone on a first visit, but I couldn't get rid of him.

"What do we do first?" he asked after the interviewers and the superintendent had left.

"Well, you could show me Classroom 305," I replied.

The room was in a remote part of the rambling school building, at the near end of a long, third-floor hallway. There's nothing quite so lonely as an empty school, and our footsteps echoed like gunshots off the polished brick

Footsteps in the Attic

walls. We stopped at the door marked "305," the principal took a set of what looked like a hundred keys, effortlessly selected one, and opened the door.

It was getting dark outside, and the room was dim. As we entered, I at once felt "heavier." There was an immediate sense of depression, to the point that I became almost dizzy. The room, about forty-five feet long and maybe thirty feet wide, with a windowed door at each end, seemed clean but uncannily dingy, almost stuffy. I switched on my gauss meter and moved slowly along the back wall, down the long outside wall with its ceiling-high windows, then along the front wall, with its long blackboard. All along that blackboard, readings fluctuated wildly, even into the negative range. There was some real magnetic-field monkey business going on here.

"Now what?" asked the principal in a quiet, nervous voice from the back of the room.

"We wait," I replied, navigating back to his side through a row of desks.

Even in cases where there are physical phenomena, it often takes hours, days or even weeks for me to actually document them, if at all. But this wasn't to be a problem in Classroom 305. The principal and I had been sitting quietly at the back of the room for about ten minutes. It was getting quite dark, and the only light came through the hallway windows at each end of the room. The only sound was the distant roar of traffic through the closed windows.

When it happened, I felt it first. Then the principal looked at me, his eyes wide. He felt it too. "Something" had arrived in the room. We both sensed it come through the door at the front of the room and move along the blackboard, then up the wall of windows toward us, then back down toward the blackboard. I glanced at my companion, who stared toward the blackboard, sweating.

There came a sharp scrape. A desk chair was moving

across the floor at the front of the room. It stopped by the door, and there came a heavy "thump" like someone pounding on the blackboard. There even was chalk dust in the air!

Fascinated, I got up and moved slowly toward the activity.

"PSSST!" came from behind. The principal gave me a pitiful look as I glanced back. He was terrified! I raised a hand in assurance and made a motion that I hoped told him I had to proceed and that he should stay put. As I moved forward again, another chair scraped, but this time it was the principal making a quick retreat through the back door!

There was another angry thump on the blackboard as I approached, then silence. I was frustrated because of the principal's fear, not a good emotion to be carrying if this turned out to be a parasite, since those critters feed on negative "vibes." Almost at once I was engulfed in a swirl of energy, and my skin tingled. This didn't feel like anger. More like frustration. This *could* be a parasite, but somehow I didn't think so. I gave it the benefit of the doubt.

"Be at peace. All will be well," I said quietly, trying to clear my mind.

Another thump, this time at the other end of the blackboard, then quick footsteps in front of the windows toward the back of the room. I wasn't getting through.

Then there was a movement by the front door. I glanced that way and froze for an instant as I caught a face staring back at me through the classroom door. It was the principal! He was breaking my concentration again! The entity was gone.

So were we. Back in his office, the principal was a wreck. I even had to follow him home after he locked the building! During the next week, I did some research and tried to isolate what I was dealing with. This being had some

Footsteps in the Attic

characteristics of a parasite – negative manifestations such as pounding and chair-moving. On the other hand, I've never found parasites operating for long in public places because there's nobody for them to attach to – people in places like that always are coming and going. Besides, I hadn't felt the non-human, cold sterility I always pick up around parasites. In my opinion, the negative emotions pointed toward a "tortured soul."

What clinched my diagnosis was some painstaking research at the city library and at the school department. I looked at the history and even the blueprints of the school, which had been built in the early 1900s. I checked the history of the area and even what I could find about its geology. I had no soil engineer working with me in those days, but I knew that the clay soil and high water table the school was built on is a combination that conducts electrical fields very well, making it all the easier for paranormal phenomena to occur. From the blueprints, I saw at once that some hefty plumbing and wiring ran past the room's front wall, just behind the blackboard.

All things considered, this room was a good candidate for slips in space-time and "ghosts from elsewhen."

I even got into some old personnel records and newspaper archives. I was about to give up on that part of it when I stumbled on the obituary of a teacher who had died in 1932 at the age of forty two in a collision between an automobile and a trolley car. Let's call her Mary Martin. Something "clicked" when I saw Mary's picture, as though I'd met her before. A little more research revealed that she not only had taught at the school, but had reigned for fifteen years over what was today Classroom 305. The principal, his wits recovered, led me to a retired janitor whom he didn't consider a security risk and who had been a student of Mary's the year she died.

"Miss Martin was totally dedicated to the school; it was her whole life. She never got married and she was a complete nervous wreck," Ted said. "She was always pacing back and forth in front of that blackboard or in front of those windows. And she was never satisfied, with us or with the room! She'd always be telling us we could do better, even if we'd get a 'B' or 'B-plus.' And she was forever moving desks and chairs around!"

Well, I saw this as a pretty good place to begin. The personality Ted described could be summed up in one word: frustration. Then came the breakthrough.

"You know, us kids never really liked that room much after she passed on, and I heard some weird stuff in there when I came back to work at the school years later."

That did it as far as I was concerned. We quite probably had met Mary Martin pacing the room in 1928 or thereabouts!

When I next spoke with the principal, school had dismissed for the year, and I strongly suggested that, starting with the 1993-1994 school year, he put the most positive teacher he could find in Room 305, even if he had to change class assignments. I realized then that it was a good thing the man had been with me that night to have the daylights scared out of him – he was all ears to my advice!

The following week, I was back in Classroom 305 — alone, this time – quietly expressing compassion and sympathy for Mary. There were no manifestations, and the atmosphere seemed a little "lighter."

With other matters competing for my time, school officials gave me the go-ahead to instruct the teachers who were going to use the room about how to project positive energy, especially compassion. It worked, from what everyone could see. During the rest of the summer, my follow-up revealed that the janitors still had some problems in the room. But when school began and teachers started projecting positive energy there, things went better, and they reported fewer and fewer incidents.

Footsteps in the Attic

School officials were delighted. One of the few who knew the details later asked me why Mary would be "stuck" in the room after she died. Must have been her violent death, right? I patiently explained that, in my opinion, Mary's presence in the room had nothing to do with her bodily death but everything to do with her life. She was still alive in the '20s or early '30s in any number of parallel universes, and in many of those she still stalked Classroom 305, fussing over her students and rearranging chairs. Given the electromagnetic site conditions, her intense dedication might have manifested through space-time for decades whether she had died or not. I have several cases in my files in which the "tortured souls" manifesting as ghosts actually turned out to be people still living in our corner of the multiverse.

Kevin and the Little Girl

By American standards, New England is a very old place. History really is alive here, and many people live in houses that remember honest Puritan farm families or periwigged gentlemen who offered toasts to King George II.

When I walk through the carven doorway of an old home in our corner of the world, I feel these people around me. And why not? In quantum reality, they are, and we're all part of each other! But their unique personal energies don't always stay in their own pocket of the multiverse, especially if they're suffering. I believe this is a frequent cause of ghost phenomena, and I believe it was the case with at least one of the ghosts at the Marshburn home in Cumberland, Rhode Island, when I got the call in early 2000.

It was my second lecture season after *Faces at the Window* appeared, and I'd recently done a book signing and presentation at the Barnes & Noble store in nearby Bellingham, Massachusetts. A friend of the Marshburns had come all the way from Leominster, Massachusetts, to be there.

"You've got to talk to this guy!" she told Bonnie Marshburn later.

When I spoke with her on the phone that first time, Bonnie didn't seem especially upset about what was going on in her home. She came across as fascinated and a little concerned.

"It's more interesting than scary," she stated. "But my husband had a real scare!"

That was where I stopped her. "Let me see for myself," I replied.

It was a cloudy day in February when I first visited the Marshburns. To my delight, I found a beautifully restored, eighteenth-century farmhouse surrounded by woods and some newer houses. And since positive people have fewer ghost problems, I was even more pleased to find a very positive couple in their forties. They had two teenagers, a boy and a girl, whom I didn't meet on that first visit.

I dropped onto a couch in the bright family room, and I was at once joined by the enormous family dog. Bonnie and her husband, John, explained that the place had an intriguing history.

"This house was a stop on the Underground Railroad in the 1850s, and we think one of the escaped slaves must have died here," John declared.

Of course, that's a story that sticks to many New England houses built before 1860 or so. Sometimes it's true, sometimes not, but the Marshburn house isn't mentioned in the town, state or national historic registers. I've never been able to verify the story.

The Marshburns had lived there for about six years. Interestingly, from what I was able to learn later, there had been a change of owners every six to eight years as far back as the 1950s.

After Bonnie signed my standard pre-investigation form, I started, as I always do, with a quiet, self-guided tour. I visited and photographed all the rooms, including an ancient cellar. The latter was cramped but not creepy. It was the living room that drew me, particularly the corner with the hutch. There was something there for sure, and it felt like a young girl.

My gauss meter registered a weak but alternating magnetic field that could have had several quite ordinary causes, but it was that clear feeling of being watched by someone shy that made me pay attention. And then there was the painting. Hanging on the living-room wall between the hutch and the front door, it was a lovely, nineteenth-century-style watercolor print of a little blonde girl. It at once reminded me of the child in Renoir's *Girl with a Watering Can*. John said he'd bought it on Cape

The painting

Cod the previous summer.

"I thought it looked just like our daughter when she was a little younger," he explained. "But I wonder if something came with it!"

What John meant was that after the painting arrived, people in the living room started to get the feeling they were – you guessed it — being watched. It wasn't threatening, the Marshburns insisted, but it was obvious. I agreed that it was almost as if someone – a little girl – was hiding behind that hutch.

Then John told me about the apparition, adjacent to the living room and between the first-floor bathroom and the master bedroom.

"I was in the bathroom late one night. When I came out to go back to bed, I saw a young, blonde-haired girl standing between me and the bedroom door. I was startled, but I assumed it was Natalie (the daughter). But then she just disappeared! Actually, she looked like the girl in the painting!"

Now here's where some alarm bells started going off. In a hefty forty percent of my cases, some little blond girl seems to pop up at some point, usually in the early stages. More often than not, it turns out to be a parasitical entity (see Part 3) or somebody from elsewhen glimpsed once or twice because of the site conditions (the electromagnetics, geotechnics and people).

At the same time, ghosts that seem attached to things are a common theme in folklore, at tourist attractions and, sometimes, in real hauntings. As I point out in the introduction to this book, matter is just another form of energy. As our consciousness spreads out in vast waves

Photo by Paul F. Eno

The orb at upper right appeared in different places in each photo. This was where the "little girl" seemed to be.

across space-time, objects we are attached to in our conscious lives go with us. When another consciousness from somewhere or somewhen else possesses the same material object, part of us quite literally goes with it. On the rare occasions when conditions are just right, the object can be a link between the two or more consciousnesses that possess it. Sometimes this can take the form of one or more ghost experiences.

This could very likely be the case with the Marshburns' painting,

I returned on March 18 with some of my team. My colleague Shane Sirois had breezed down from New Hampshire that morning. Also on hand were soil engineer Joe Frisella and electrical-engineering professor Everett Crisman.

Bonnie and John talked with Shane and me while Joe and Everett checked the outside of the house and the land around it. The first thing Shane and I always do is try to determine what we're dealing with, and it's the trickiest part of any investigation! Unlike most investigators, I never assume that something *is* what it *looks like* because we know that parasites can act perfectly innocent.

As we progressed in the Marshburn case, however, I became sure that we were dealing with at least one "ghost from elsewhen" but no parasites.

While Shane and I wrestled with that little issue, Joe and Everett looked at site soil composition and its possibilities for electrical conductivity. We find that most houses with paranormal goings-on are built on moist, sandy or clay soils with high water tables. Joe noticed right away that the Marshburn lot was most likely one of these.

We also checked the outside and found an active magnetic field, something many researchers refer to as an energy vortex, in the area of the kitchen garden and a large oak tree. Sure enough, family members reported seeing balls of light or orbs in that area from time to time.

Back in the living room, I still felt that little-girl presence, so out came the digital camera. The first shot clearly

Photo by Paul F. Eno

Looking through the chinks into "Kevin's" secret cellar.

Footsteps in the Attic

showed an orb just above the hutch on the upper left. Just to be sure it wasn't a glitch, I took another shot, and there was an orb again, this time on the right.

I'm not convinced one way or the other what orbs actually are. I've had them appear in pictures for years, and I've seen them with my own eyes. They've appeared in different colors, and I've even had them act in quite an intelligent manner, interacting – even seeming to play – with each other, and following me, then retreating as I attempted to follow them.

Just when I convince myself that orbs must be related to ball lightning or some other electrical phenomenon, they do something maddeningly ghostly, such as showing up with a face in them, as on the cover of this book. Still, I hesitate to say that they're actually ghosts. In tune with my other theories, I venture that they're something of both – electrical phenomena that tie in with our own – or others' – electrical properties and then manifest accordingly. Daughter Natalie Marshburn, apparently the most psychic or energy-perceptive member of the family, had seen orbs upstairs.

But the real question was: What was this little girl doing behind the Marshburns' hutch? A psychic friend the Marshburns consulted before me had, of course, a Victorian séance-room idea quite different from mine.

"She told us that there is a little girl here. She died of a lung illness, maybe pneumonia, and that her parents' grief is what's held her on Earth," Bonnie reported.

Well, here we went with the death thing again.

"I don't think it quite works that way," I explained. "I think she's very much alive in her world and is simply connected with yours, perhaps through her love of the painting. I don't think she's necessarily the one *in* the painting, but I believe she sees and feels us the same way we see and feel her, at least at times. Sure, she may have died of pneumonia in a million parallel worlds, but that's not why she's manifesting here. I feel her curiosity, not her pain."

As a matter of fact, somewhere or somewhen else, this probably was the kid's house and she was nervous about *our* presence! But before the end of that day, we seemed to have a double-header on our hands.

"We should show you the 'secret cellar,'" Bonnie said suddenly.

The house indeed had two cellars, and I'd seen only the smaller one on my first visit. Descending into the depths from the only entrance, an outdoor bulkhead, I felt as though I were sliding into a completely different world. It was a larger cellar, lined with rough fieldstones by some long-gone colonial hands. Here was no feeling of childish curiosity. This was the electrical tingle, the pain and depression I'd picked up during some of my most memorable cases.

This, apparently, was someone other than our little girl, and no-one in our group felt comfortable after this first meeting.

"We believe this is where the escaped slaves hid, and we think one of them died here. We think he's buried in there," John declared, pointing toward another fieldstone wall. Pointing our flashlights through a few large gaps in the stonework, we saw the "secret cellar," a completely bare dirt floor with yet another wall of fieldstones beyond.

Shane and I took some photos, none of which contained any obvious anomalies. We finally left, knowing that the case had taken on a new depth.

Back home, I thought deeply about this new development, and it bothered me that the case seemed unclear.

With all my scientific – some might say pseudo-scientific – theories and pronouncements, it may come as a surprise that I very occasionally use an unusual tool that quite literally dropped into my life many years ago. As a

Footsteps in the Attic

child, I spent a great deal of time with an aunt who had been deeply influenced by the Cherokee spirituality and way of life. That's a long story, but suffice it to say that my own spirituality had a strong Native American influence long before the "New Agers" made that trendy.

The tool I refer to is a simple "medicine staff," a long, uncarved piece of wood with a flattened knob at the top. It literally dropped at my feet one day when I was walking behind our old house in Cumberland, the very town in which the Marshburns lived. Presumably, this staff, just short of six feet long, fell from the steep slope above. But who knows?

Wherever it came from, I quickly found that if I rested this staff on the ground or floor and placed my forehead against the flattened part, it focused my thoughts and insights. From time to time, I've even been able to grab images from elsewhen that have done people some good.

As you can see from this book's appendix on Ouija boards and séances, I'm extremely wary about this sort of thing, so I use this staff very sparingly. Still, I don't believe I'm contacting spirits. The staff simply seems to be a very personal tool that can concentrate my own powers of connection, seemingly to other areas of space-time, to gain better insight now and then.

About a week after the "secret cellar" visit, I was doing my evening rule of prayer when the medicine staff, which I keep leaning against my home altar, suddenly slid over and hit me gently on my side. That had never happened before and it hasn't since.

Subtle as a ton of bricks, I thought. I put the staff top to my forehead then and there. The impressions started coming, clear, searing and immediate: Pain. Suffering. Tortured soul. Kevin.

The next day, I was on the phone with Bonnie, and she seemed spellbound as I explained what had happened.

"This may seem like a strange question," she said suddenly, "but did you get a name?"

"Kevin," I replied.

"My God! That's what she said his name is!"

"She" turned out to be the family's psychic friend, whom Bonnie had talked with after my last visit. As it turned out, the girl's brother had owned the house at one time and her sister-in-law had had ghost trouble.

Well, ghosts – at least the ones that aren't parasites – are people, too. And what do we do for people we can't help in any other way? We pray.

"He's alive and in trouble somewhere in space-time, Bonnie. I don't know if he's an escaped slave or what. That doesn't matter. Pray for him. Have the family pray for him. Think about him with compassion. Send out love for him whenever you're in the house."

As recently as a decade ago, I'd immediately charge into houses like the Marshburns' with clergy, crosses and holy water. But that didn't always work. What did work, and works every time as long as the people in the house co-operate, is simply love. Corny as it may sound, love – the most positive energy of all – can heal the wounds of all those around us, whether it's our family and friends here and now or fellow humans suffering elsewhere in the multiverse.

Sure enough, I was touched and delighted to hear what Bonnie had to say when I made a follow-up phone call some time later.

"We prayed for Kevin, and we asked all our friends to," she related with some emotion. "And you know, not long afterward, Natalie came down one morning and told us she'd had the most wonderful dream. She said she'd been gently rocking in a hammock under the tree in the back yard – where you said the vortex was. She looked up and she knew it was Kevin rocking her. She said he had the most beautiful smile and the happiest eyes!"

All seems well at the Marshburn house. Now they're

Footsteps in the Attic

working for the little girl, and there are no plans to move! I don't think the tyke is a "tortured soul," but only good can come from expressing love, so why not?

People who hear about the Marshburn case often ask, "Wouldn't you have to excavate the 'secret cellar,' find Kevin's body and give it a proper burial?"

"This isn't a TV show," I usually reply. "This is reality!"

What does it matter where your body is buried? After all, you have millions of them scattered through space-time! What matters is the love and the connection with our fellow creatures of good will. That's what feeds life and that's what gives peace.

Wherever and whenever Kevin was suffering, I like to think that the Marshburns' love has helped give him joy instead.

Footsteps in the Attic

3

THE PARASITES

There's a line from the hit 1982 film *Poltergeist* in which the little psychic tells the frightened mom: "It knows what scares you."

She was right.

The parasites: I run into them all the time. They're hungry and they're hostile, and in my experience they're partners with their unwitting victims in the most negative ghost phenomena, especially poltergeists. But they also can appear completely benign – at first. In a number of my cases, what I first thought were "ghosts from elsewhen" or "tortured souls" have turned out to be parasites fishing for victims.

I can't say precisely what sort of lifeforms these parasites are or just where or when they come from in the multiverse. But they seem to be able to "drop in" on our corner of space-time whenever the energies (both geotechnic and biological) are just right. There may be many varieties or species. They feed off negative emotions, they learn, they get stronger, and they know just what human "buttons" to push to get the most to "eat."

Whenever I go head to head with them, I don't feel anything human. I very rarely see them (when I do, they look like tall streaks of electricity or plasma) and I've been able to photograph one only a few times in my thirty-plus years of paranormal research. But when I investigate a site where they've been operating, I feel them right away, and their presence can be overwhelming. They come across to me as cold, sterile, uncaring and usually hostile, but sometimes fearful. And yes, I would go so far as to call them "alien" in whatever way you might interpret that.

Here are some of their characteristics:

· They nearly always start weakly (footsteps in the attic, for example), then get stronger as people get more alarmed. For months or even years, they may manifest as harmless, stereotypical ghosts or other spirits.

Footsteps in the Attic

· Parasites often will take on the characteristics, personality traits and even the physical appearance of their victims. I believe that some people can project personalities onto parasites.

· Some parasites are worse than others. For example, some work on their victims until they get enough energy to become poltergeists, tulpas or both. Others seem satisfied to "eat light" and manifest only once in a while.

· They all seem able to "fade" in and out of our corner of quantum reality, but many seem attached to – or have their only access through — the place people encounter them.

· Some seem to already be there when the victim arrives on the scene. These, I find, almost always are attached to the site – or at least are very limited in their mobility in our part of the multiverse — because of the factors (such as a site's geomagnetic energies) that allow them to manifest in our reality. If one victim at such a site wises up, gets positive and defeats the parasite, it often will try to attach itself to the next likely person there.

· Some parasites can give the impression of being male or female.

· A few I've encountered seem more "mobile," with entities able to stay attached to victims even if the latter move from place to place. Some even seem attached to families for generations at a stretch, but this is rare.

· Parasites are drawn by occult activities, especially séances and Ouija boards, because these can literally punch holes in space-time.

· They seem to pick on vulnerable people, especially women and young people who have been abused.

· As far as I know, nobody has ever researched the health effects of paranormal parasite experiences. It seems to me that their victims can suffer negative, sometimes very negative, health consequences. I've seen everything from chronic fatigue syndrome to suicide that I believe were caused, at least indirectly, by parasites.

· Just as people have different personalities, so do parasites. Most are pretty nasty, but a few seem less so, being satisfied with "lighter fare" by playing pranks or stirring people up in other ways.

· They can be beaten when people replace negative energy with positive energy in their lives and homes. People need support from friends and loved ones to do so.

What kind of lifeforms could these be?

The great astronomer Sir Fred Hoyle believed that life is the rule in the universe, not the exception. Life is everywhere, even in the most impossible environments, he stated. He cited microbes found in the cores of nuclear reactors and on meteors newly arrived from space. He mentioned the bizarre lifeforms recently discovered around volcanic vents in the ocean floor in places sunlight never reaches. He even pointed to the vast interstellar clouds of what most of his fellow astronomers believe are gas. Sir Fred was convinced that these aren't composed of gas at all, but are masses of microbes! Whenever there has been an explosion of genetic mutations and new life forms on Earth, such as in the Cambrian period half a billion years ago, Sir Fred believed that the planet had passed through one of these clouds, and that microbes filtered through the atmosphere into the ecosystem.

I think Sir Fred had a point. Look into any hole in the world — on land or at the bottom of the sea – and you'll find some form of life. Why shouldn't there be life unimagined in the quantum holes *between* the worlds? I believe this can begin to explain what sort of lifeforms parasites are.

Science fiction? Not on your life. I think this is as real as it gets.

The vampire factor

I think these parasitical entities are responsible for the demons, mischievous spirits and other supernatural menaces of folklore. Any good student of folklore learns to take it seriously. That's because every legend, no matter how silly to modern ears, has some grain of truth at its root. Take, for example, the very earliest legends of vampires – we're talking thousands of years, back to the ancient Middle East and China. These legends from the remote past weren't about blood-sucking European noblemen. They were about life-sucking ghosts. And since "blood is life," as it says in Genesis 9:6 and Deuteronomy 12:33, Europeans eventually came to think of vampires as blood suckers.

I believe that the parasitic entities I encounter are the life-sucking ghosts of primal human folklore. The good news is that they can be sent packing, or at least kept under control, sometimes without all that much difficulty.

Can they be human?

People often ask me why I'm so convinced that at least some parasites aren't human. After all, they say, plenty of humans are like "psychic vampires" and lots of human relationships are parasitical. Why can't parasitical people end up in parallel universes where they can prey on us?

I freely admit that this is possible and even makes a certain amount of sense. But I must say that in all my years of research, I've never encountered a parasite (a paranormal one, anyway) that I honestly thought was human. Even when they pretend to be, say, your late Uncle George, their nature invariably turns nasty and alien the more energy they draw from their victims.

So while there may be human parasitical entities, I don't believe that I've ever encountered one.

Footsteps in the Attic

IDing parasites

As I've mentioned, one of my first tasks in any case is to find out whether I'm dealing with a parasite. This is just what most investigators *don't* look for. I find that many ghosts that come across as "tortured souls" actually are parasites looking for a "meal." This becomes clear when the phenomena begin to get negative, especially when people aggravate it by serving themselves up as a smorgasbord in a séance or by using a Ouija board.

Someone in distress somewhere or somewhen else generally isn't going to start threatening people or tossing dishes around in someone else's universe. They're too wrapped up in what's happening to them in their own world, or the power of their emotions wouldn't be jackhammering through space-time.

As in all cases, I look very carefully at the people. Have they been involved in occult activities that can open holes in space-time and attract parasites? Do they complain of feeling tired and drained? Are they undergoing tough times or family disharmony? Most importantly, are they telling me the whole story?

You'd be surprised how many parasite victims actually like the attention and excitement the situation brings. I've encountered a few lonely souls who actually have bonded with a parasite (yuck)!

The poltergeist

At the extreme end of the line is the poltergeist, which certainly makes it easy to decide whether there's a parasite involved. "Poltergeist" derives from two German words meaning "noisy spirit." That's putting it mildly. I've seen poltergeists pick people up, start fires, throw furniture around and break windows. A few have thrown things at me, and I was once injured by a flying television.

Nobody knows for sure how poltergeists do what they

do, but I'd say the controversial Hutchison Effect is a good candidate. The Hutchison Effect is very complex. It's basically an anti-gravity phenomenon that has to do with electromagnetic fields, zero-point energy, quantum vacuum, radio waves, a high-voltage power source and two or three Tesla coils. Supposedly, it can even change levitated objects' molecular structure. One British writer has referred to the Hutchison Effect as the "poltergeist machine."

It's controversial because nobody seems able to replicate the effects produced, and recorded on film, by Canadian researcher John Hutchison in 1979. Though some of his experiments supposedly were witnessed and videotaped by scientists and military officials, other researchers have questioned everything from Hutchison's record-keeping to his honesty.

Any critic who had been with me during the Bridgeport, Connecticut, poltergeist case of 1974 (see *Faces at the Window*, New River Press, 1998), when city policeman and I watched televisions, tables, chairs and a refrigerator floating around, might have found the experience educational and Hutchison's work well worth pursuing.

What to do?

For many years I'd go barreling into poltergeist cases and other negative paranormal situations with clergy and religious objects. It didn't always work. But as early as the late 1970s, it was dawning on me that the kind of people involved in a case seemed directly related to the kind of phenomena: The more negative the people and their situation, the more negative the phenomena.

So I started trying something simple: "Out with the bad air; in with the good." I started encouraging negative people to get positive and to fill their homes with positive energy, especially love. And wouldn't you know, it worked – and it's been working ever since.

John Lennon was right: "All you need is love!"

The Baddest Poltergeist in New England

Ironically, the worst poltergeist I ever faced was the easiest to get rid of. It was March 1979 when a frantic call came from Steve Cargill, a friend of mine in New Haven, Connecticut.

"Even you won't believe this one!" Steve was yelling. I could hear banging and hollering in the background.

"What?" I shouted back, alarmed.

"The craziest poltergeist you ever saw! I'm there now!"

Fortunately, I was still living in East Hartford, about thirty-five miles to the north, so I wasn't far away. I dropped everything and headed for New Haven. Following Steve's hasty directions, I soon found myself at the back door of a good-sized, "mom and pop" convenience store not far from the city line. There was a big "closed" sign at the front door, and the store windows all were curtained. I'd been told to slink around to the rear door as invisibly as I could. I knocked, then jumped back when the door opened immediately.

"Are you Paul?" asked a big, forty-something woman.

"Yes, ma'am," I responded.

Without another word, her arm shot out, grabbed my sleeve and pulled me in. She looked exhausted, but her strength was alarming! The door slammed to with the nervous rustle of Venetian blinds. Before she hustled me through another door and up a flight of stairs, I had enough time to see that the darkened store was a shambles. Everything that should have been on the shelves seemed to be on the floor. There was an unpleasant smell, and I could have sworn that I saw a bottle of soda suspended high in the air over the middle aisle.

"Up this way. This is where it's worst," my apparent hostess pointed up the stairs, which were littered with articles of clothing. At the top, a spacious apartment opened out. The place would have been beautiful had it

Footsteps in the Attic

not been an absolute catastrophe. The floor was covered with debris, there were black scrawls of "death," "die" and a few less mentionable things on the walls, and the place reeked of sulphur. The electrical field was so powerful that it felt like bugs crawling all over my skin.

"This is my home! Do you believe this? Ahhhhh!!" She shrieked, and my head quickly swung around to look where she was looking. We both ducked just in time as a huge armchair whizzed over our heads and crashed against the opposite wall!

"What now?" came a shout from the bathroom, and Steve stumbled out, still fastening his pants. "Oh, you're here!" he picked his way across the room to shake my hand nervously. Somehow I felt free to skip my usual "Is this really paranormal?" process.

"All right!" I stated with a glance over each shoulder. "What's the story?"

At once something started to pound on the floors right beneath our feet. I had just turned to run back down the stairs to see what it was when the woman, whose name turned out to be Liz Centracci, shouted over the din: "Don't bother. It's the ghost."

Well, it seems that "the ghost" had been raising the devil at this scene off and on for over a year.

"A year?" I blurted in amazement.

It's unusual for a poltergeist to last more than three months at a stretch. The longest documented case I'm aware of was at Kuokkaniemi in Finland, and that went on for a little less than three years, beginning in 1900. It's also unusual for a poltergeist to keep going flat-out when I arrive. Usually things calm down for awhile, seemingly until it gets "used" to me and my own electrical field, introduced into its "mix."

The thing was quiet long enough for me to hear the whole tale.

Liz had been a widow for about five years. Her husband had left her the once-prosperous little store beneath our feet, and a very decent chunk of money. That was good, because Liz had their little girl to bring up. Things had gone pretty well until early 1978, when pounding had started on the floor of the apartment, seeming to move rapidly around underneath. In the store below, the pounding was on the ceiling, of course, and Liz would tell customers hastily that she was having some repair work done.

On the sly, she had the place checked for mice, rats, termites and every other physical pest known to man. She sought help from utility companies and even consulted a seismologist from nearby Yale University, all to no avail. Phenomena kept getting worse and, within six months, Liz had to close the store – after something started throwing bottles of soda at customers one day. That's how she had met Steve.

"I happened to be in the store about six months ago, and I got beaned by a bottle of ginger ale!" he recalled. "There was nobody else in the store, and Liz seemed real nervous. I 'put two and two together' and told her I knew a guy who worked with 'weird stuff.' I left her my phone number."

Meanwhile, Liz told customers that she was closing the store to start a major remodeling project. She even had her brother-in-law, a contractor, park one of his trucks outside a few days a week. But if anybody was going to do some remodeling, it was the space-time beast inside.

By mid-1978, voices had joined the pounding. Liz and her fourteen year-old daughter, Anna, would hear each other speaking even when both weren't present. Not long after that, apparitions began, getting more terrifying by the week: faces bobbing in the air, black shadows creeping across the floor and through the air, both in the store and the apartment, and red eyes seen peering from beneath furniture.

Footsteps in the Attic

That's when Liz packed the frazzled Anna off to her sister-in-law's in nearby East Haven. But Liz, a sort of Annie Oakley of the paranormal, was determined to fight it out. She would take "breathers" from time to time, staying with Anna and her sister-in-law for a few days just to get her strength back. Courageous and cavalier as Liz was, things only got worse when she went back to the apartment and the parasite started sucking her energy again.

After awhile, Liz wasn't able sleep in the apartment at all, and she moved in with her sister-in-law and daughter. But nearly every morning, Liz would be back in her domain to keep watch and battle the poltergeist, almost as though she were going to work. Of course, all she was doing was feeding the thing. Liz told me that it would take the beast a good hour to get revved up after she arrived in the morning. In fact, she was a sort of human cup of coffee for it.

Down in the shuttered store, what was left of the stock wouldn't stay on the shelves, and Liz finally gave up trying to keep it there. About two months before I showed up, the black scrawls had started appearing on walls and ceilings in the apartment, and the poltergeist began literally knocking holes in the walls.

The real trouble here was that Liz had done everything wrong from day one, right down to the last detail. She and a friend had been playing with a Ouija board for weeks before the trouble began. Obviously, something unpleasant came through. Later, when phenomena got worse, Liz became convinced that it was a ghost and organized a séance with a local medium and a few trusted friends. This just took what the Ouija board had done and made it worse. I later met two of Liz's friends who had attended, and they confirmed that "the voice of an angry young woman" had come through the medium, claiming she had been murdered in a house on that spot in 1820 and wanted revenge. It was the usual nonsense parasites dish out to get their victims stirred up. The spot had been the middle of a cornfield in 1820, at least in our corner of quantum reality.

The medium never came back.

Liz's solution had been to alternately shout at the poltergeist, then ignore it. She sprinkled holy water or salt, burned incense and otherwise called upon every folk remedy she could find in books at the local branch of the New Haven Free Public Library.

It's not that these methods don't work, but they work much better when done with faith and a positive spirit than with fear and superstition. That's because they're tools: They have little power in themselves, but they can concentrate and energize the power of our own minds to positively take control our own environment. But the tools must fit the user. Crosses rarely work for non-Christians, for example, but I've seen teddy bears work as protective tools for children. It really does depend on the person. Liz was using her chosen tools in fear and anger.

All this hullabaloo provided more energy for the original parasite, *and* attracted some of its buddies. In my initial investigation, when I wasn't dodging flying furniture, I felt strongly that there were at least six parasites having a field day, not only in the apartment but also in the store below.

In a situation that would have sent most people packing long before, Liz got more and more determined. But as her anger grew, it too fed the parasites. And as she continued to live off her savings, without income from the store, she got more and more worried, and *that* fed the parasites.

I've seen this circle-the-wagons mentality many times, though not for so long a period. Homeowners and even renters have a certain primal instinct to defend their homes. I've often seen people stick it out even on the

Footsteps in the Attic

rare occasions I've advised them to move. Of course, phenomena at Liz's weren't constant. Poltergeists tend to be active for a few days or a week, then re-energize before getting active again. So Liz did have a period of relative quiet every week or so. But nothing she could do seemed to bring the trouble to an end.

Finally, she dug out Steve's number and called him.

Liz struck me as not only strong but also honest, at least beyond the remodeling fib. For example, she was a Roman Catholic, but she hadn't called her priest because she was afraid he'd be upset about her using Ouija boards and doing séances. The idea of simply not telling him the truth evidently hadn't occurred to her. Actually, it probably was just as well that she didn't call in clergy. People often are shocked when I say that few clergy are educated about the paranormal, but it's true. At times, they can do more harm than good.

A real miracle of this case was that Liz managed to keep the information lid on the situation. I found all sorts of rumors flying around the neighborhood, what with the store closing, Anna leaving and all sorts of odd noises. The general belief was that Liz had gone a little batty, couldn't be bothered with the store anymore and was living off a huge inheritance. The fact that nobody who had seen anything in the store or apartment seems to have talked about it, probably for fear of sounding crazy, was a minor miracle in itself.

It was a good thing for all concerned that the media never got hold of this. With the Bridgeport poltergeist outbreak only a few years before, reporters would have loved it! If Liz had called the police, one of the first things most poltergeist victims do, the media would have found out for sure.

Of course, press photographers might have been as frustrated as I was by one thing: During the entire course of the case, not a single one of my photos came out! It was the only time this has ever happened.

It was a good thing, too, that poltergeists don't last forever. Sooner or later, they get all the energy they can from their victim, and they start to weaken. This rat pack got weaker, I'm convinced, simply because even the gallant Liz was starting to wear down. By the time I took over the case, these "noisy spirits" were near the end of their electromagnetic ropes anyway.

I suggested calling in an Eastern Orthodox priest I knew to at least bless the house, but he wasn't available. Since I realized the parasites were playing themselves out and because I already was starting to form my "out with the bad air, in with the good" theory, I was convinced that Liz, Steve and I could get rid of them ourselves.

So that evening, after we'd gotten Liz out of the apartment for a decent meal, we all marched straight back in. All was quiet as we stood in the middle of the floor and held hands. We said the Lord's Prayer, and I announced calmly to the parasites that we had their number, that the game was up, and that Liz wasn't going to be their meal ticket anymore, or words to that effect.

There was a thump under our feet that shook the floor, but I had told Liz and Steve to remain calm at all cost. That night, I convinced Liz to stay with her sister-in-law until we had pacified the situation. The next day and the next, Steve, Liz and I were back. We did everything positive we could think of. We read from the happier parts of the Bible, we shared stories about our families and our happy memories, and we even had a great evening reading from a joke book and singing songs. On the last evening, we had Anna with us, and she seemed completely renewed afterward.

That really did it. I checked with Liz often over the next two months, and Steve stopped by frequently. She and Anna, who moved back home, had cleaned up the apartment within the week and had repairs done. Within a

Footsteps in the Attic

month, the store was open again, and it didn't take long for things to get back to normal.

As far as I know, Liz never had trouble again. The key was that she kept that positive spirit and broke her link in the chain of factors that can permit paranormal phenomena of this kind to take place. With the love of her daughter and her home, she won the victory that anger never could.

Carmen's Spirit

People often ask which of my cases was the most frightening. They expect me to answer that it was some poltergeist that threw me through a window or set fire to my pants. They're surprised when I reply that the scariest cases often are the quietest. They're the ones in which the victims actually develop a relationship with the parasite.

Of course, the whole situation must be shaken down for psychiatric or other "natural" causes before concluding that there's a parasite at work. But when there is, these cases can be horrible! For victim and investigator both, reality can literally become blurred as universes blend and victims experience intensely personal, vampire-like encounters with parasites, with which they may develop close, co-dependent or even erotic relationships.

Frankly, I'd rather have an honest poltergeist throw a refrigerator at me than have to plunge in and try to disentangle one of these sick, paranormal relationships. It's almost always a lengthy process. Unfortunately, such relationships occur all too often in cases that involve parasites.

In my experience, the most common victim is the weak, vulnerable, insecure person – usually a woman – who has a history of being abused or otherwise victimized. I'm reminded quite chillingly of the old vampire stories, with the master recruiting his victim-slaves one by one, then feeding from them until he can get no more.

The other most frequent parasite prey is the person who seeks power over others through the occult. In deliberately trying to link up with sometimes hostile powers elsewhere in the multiverse, this sort literally invites trouble and usually gets it. In trying to use these forces to control others, he or she usually ends up being controlled, or at least harmed mentally and spiritually. Sometimes self-harm or even suicide result.

These relationships may be relatively common among parasite cases, but I've dealt with few of them over the years because victims usually don't realize they have a problem until they wind up in psychiatric treatment or worse.

Fortunately, Carmen Kerrigan was an exception: She had enough horse sense to know that something wasn't right, and as the relationship with her parasite developed, she started to realize that there was more to this than there seemed to be. It was Carmen's friend and confidant Jane Gagnon who first contacted me after reading a story about me in a Rhode Island newspaper.

It was on a sunny October morning in 1998 that I first visited the house in Burrillville, Rhode Island. Jane and her two children, eight and thirteen years of age, had rented the nondescript, two-story house for two years. The thirty-ish Carmen, the confused victim of a recently failed marriage, had moved in with the family about two months before.

As usual, I took the grand tour before sitting down with the women to hear the whole tale, and it didn't take long for me to start picking up impressions. The home's layout was circular. Entering through the back door, one would move through a small living room, into the kitchen, around to a small family room, then to the bottom of the stairs. All I had to do was start up those stairs and I was awash in a hefty electrical field. Upstairs, this field was strongest in a bedroom in the northwest corner of the house. To my alarm, I found that this room belonged to Jane's eight year-old. Needless to say, I don't want to see paranormal phenomena of a negative kind anywhere near children!

Measurements with my gauss meter revealed a fluctuating magnetic field moving about upstairs, but concentrated in the child's room. All was quiet, but there, especially at the room's east wall, I got the very strong impression of an entity with male energies.

The basement seemed as clean as a whistle, paranormally speaking, but I saw that about half of it was much older than the rest of the house. A little research showed that the original house had burned in the 1950s and that the current structure stood on the old foundation. And no, nobody was killed in the fire!

The attic, to which neither Jane nor Carmen said they had ever been, was interesting. It was empty and unfinished, but I had no doubt that something was up there. Sure enough, a photograph revealed a shimmery substance in the air to one side. I believe it was the parasite and, as the case progressed, it often seemed to "hide out" in this attic when I was in the house.

Seeing no evidence of ordinary electrical problems or any other mundane cause, I gradually admitted that there really was something paranormal going on. But was it a "tortured soul" or a parasite? I gave it the benefit of the doubt.

Photo by Paul F. Eno

The space at left is shimmery in this shot of Carmen's attic, where the parasite seems to have spent time when not feeding on her.

Footsteps in the Attic

"Don't fear. All will be well," I said to the not-so-empty air upstairs. Frankly, I wasn't sure about that at all.

Gathered at the kitchen table on that first visit, Jane and Carmen told me their story.

"I think I've always known there was, you know, somebody else here. But it never really bothered me and the boys," she told me. "When I first moved in, there seemed to be a lot of activity, but at first I blew it off as old-house sounds."

Still, with all the footsteps she heard late at night, Jane came to call the entity "the walker." All the sounds seemed concentrated at the end of the house where I'd picked up the strongest impressions. As first, Jane said, she thought it was one of her sons on unauthorized absence from bed. But every effort to catch one or another boy walking around the upstairs hallway proved fruitless.

"I thought I was going nuts," she recalled, as do so many people who encounter the paranormal.

Neither Jane nor the boys "connected" with whatever this was, however, so it tended to remain in the background. But things really started to hop when Carmen moved in.

"The sounds picked up, and we felt a strong presence, not only upstairs but in the kitchen. In the living room, it even seemed like 'he' would fool around with the TV and the VCR!" Jane said.

"Aha," I said to myself. "Good old electromagnetic energy: always most obvious in rooms with plumbing and appliances!"

And there were apparitions of a man of undetermined age, always shadowy. Carmen, especially, reported seeing a man's shadow in the kitchen, upstairs and at the bottom of the stairs. Something would sit on the edge of her bed. What I found most alarming were her reports of waking in the middle of the night with the feeling of being choked by cold fingers.

In response to my long list of questions, I learned that Carmen had been under psychiatric counseling for clinical depression and hadn't been working regularly for some time. I could see right away that a sort of love-hate feeling toward the entity, real or imagined, had taken root during her long days alone in the house. Carmen called it "a conflict." She truly had "connected" with this entity in a way that Jane and the boys never had.

Jane herself seemed to take a Pollyanna approach: She wanted to believe that this was a "protective" spirit. It seemed, fortunately, to leave the eight-year-old alone, even though I often could feel it in the child's room, where the quantum "door" to the parasite's own universe seemed to be.

I was particularly interested to hear of both women's interest in the paranormal, and to see that Native American religious articles decorated several rooms. Both claimed they hadn't used Ouija boards or séances in the house, but both said they relied on the advice of a Tarot card reader. That's "iffy" at best and dangerous at worst because we know neither where the advice actually comes from nor whether it's harmful. Never take advice from any source without question!

As a protective measure, Jane was burning sage in the house, a Native American method I've used myself as a way to help dissipate negative energy. In addition to this, I urged Carmen to use the protective technique of visualizing herself surrounded by light. And before I concluded that this was a parasite, I advised her to communicate compassion and sympathy to the entity.

Given Carmen's clinical situation and the fact that she at first appeared to be the only witness to the most negative phenomena, I was immediately suspicious that she was hallucinating, or at least embellishing on a situation with an entity that might not be as threatening as it

Footsteps in the Attic

seemed. One of the first things I did was to call her psychiatric social worker, whom I found very receptive. She gave me a general picture of Carmen's situation without breaching confidentiality. Apparently, Carmen had no known condition that would have predisposed her to hallucinations.

Later, after reading my book *Faces at the Window*, which had been published that year, the counselor commented that I was more skeptical about the paranormal than she!

Later testimony by Jane, her older son, and her and Carmen's respective ex-husbands convinced me that Carmen probably wasn't imagining things. Over the next several weeks, with some intensive interviews, site visits, and photographic analysis, here's how the picture *would have* shaped up if I were a garden-variety ghost hunter:

It looked for all the world as though this entity was a "tortured soul" who was Carmen's lover in a past life. Frustrated and confused, the fellow was running around in limbo because he had apparently killed her in that past life and was dripping with guilt. Carmen even had written a love poem to the thing!

But the critter's biggest problem was that I didn't buy that story.

In quantum reality there is no time as such, hence there are no past lives. There are, of course, parallel lives that may be in one time or another, but in none of them do "tortured souls" drill into our realm and try to strangle people, at least not in my experience. Carmen's personal history, added to the negative interaction with this entity, had parasite written all over it. There were the shadowy apparitions, too, which nearly always have meant parasites in my cases.

I found it especially interesting that "the man" and Carmen had similar characteristics: frustration, depression and guilt. Once again, that's common when parasites imitate their victims. As if that weren't enough, the jobless Carmen had been cooped up and brooding in that house since moving in, also making her easy pickings for a parasite. Carmen complained of feeling tired and drained, a symptom of depression, yes, but also a clue that a parasite might be in action.

This wasn't as much of an "emergency" as some parasite cases, as there wasn't a wild poltergeist juggling armchairs. So as Carmen and I worked on "thinking positive," I had a rare chance to study this entity. I would sit for long periods in the child's room, where it seemed to "hang out," literally in or near the east wall. After it got used to me, it would flee to the attic less and less. In that bedroom, each of us knew the other was there. It felt as though we were studying each other, and I got the feeling that it knew it couldn't get anything to "eat" from me.

I felt sharp, cold intelligence. I felt that it was very old and very alien. And I knew that it was either imitating Carmen's own characteristics or reflecting the personality Carmen was projecting onto it. Either way, it had been able to win her sympathy and build her trust.

On two occasions, I was fascinated to feel the entity in my car with me as I left Carmen's and Jane's house and headed the ten miles to my own. As I suspected, however, it wasn't powerful enough to leave the hefty electromagnetic fields around its home for long. Even before I got out of Burrillville, the entity always dissipated.

I brought in soil engineer Joe Frisella, who pointed out that the site was very sandy and at the bottom of a hill. Without doing any expensive drilling, he suggested that the water table probably was quite high. Those two circumstances can contribute to a site's electrical conductivity, one of the "ducks" that must be lined up for paranormal phenomena to take place.

The plot thickened that October. Carmen called me one

Footsteps in the Attic

day to say that she had suddenly gone into a light trance and done what is known in paranormal research as "automatic writing," writing done allegedly under the control of a spirit. What resulted appears to be a conversation between Carmen and the entity. Carmen's part of the dialogue leans right, the entity's supposed answers lean left.

Bear in mind that this was written *after* I'd suggested that it *looked* like a parallel-life love connection and *after* I'd taken the attic photo shown in this chapter.

Carmen: What is bothering you?

Entity: I'm not sure. My back hurts.

Carmen: Did you know that the pain in your back is but a symptom of something much deeper?

Entity: Yes, I'm aware of that.

Carmen: What are you doing right now?

Entity: Just sitting here listening and feeling the music.

Carmen: So what do you think?

Entity: I like it but sometimes I feel sad. It touches me somehow in a way I'm not familiar with.

Carmen: Are you angry at me?

Entity: No, but you remind me. Your being here reminds me of my (illegible). It reminds me of the whole (sic) I have here, its much like yours.

Carmen: So why did you want to choke me?

Entity: Because you reminded me of her and it never stops hurting. I wander and I walk to try not to feel as that would go but it doesn't go away.

Carmen: Can you tell me about what it looks like where you are?

Entity: It was sunny at one time. It was bright and filled with laughter but that's gone now. Now its gray and cold and my heart can find no warmth so I walk.

Carmen: What else would you like to talk about? Do you believe I could help you in some way?

Footsteps in the Attic

Entity: I don't know what else to say. I don't know how you think you could help. Its been this way for so long. I don't see that I have any other choice. I don't like to talk about it or anything. I just feel so bad and so angry. I have to walk.

Carmen: I understand that sadness, the whole deep inside. I call it the soul. It gets lonely here, too.

Entity: That's why I get angry because you remind me and I don't want to be reminded. It hurts too deep. I was O.K. for a long time, a very long time but you came and now I remember....

Carmen: I keep wanting to ask you, what is in the attic?

Entity: It's the angry place. It's the late place. It's a place where I had to be so long ago but it wasn't there in the way you saw in the picture. It wasn't empty but it was never not an angry place. I could go there when I got angry. I thought it would be safe for me to be there so I wouldn't hurt anyone.

Carmen: Now I'm getting scared. O.K. I'll stop. He doesn't want to talk anymore. He's getting angry and I got scared so I walked out. I still sense the anger. I overstepped too far.

I noticed at once that Carmen and her paranormal pen pal made the same spelling and grammatical errors. A handwriting expert later told me that the same person had written the entire piece. Often in automatic writing, if that's what this was, that's not the result of the analysis. I found it curious that Carmen, who never stopped believing that this was the spirit of a dead man, never asked the entity its name or when it claimed to have lived in the house. I also thought the entity's supposed answers sounded awfully modern.

In his attic reference, it would seem that the entity had been peeping at my case pictures! I had, of course, been showing them to Carmen and Jane all along.

Throughout this period, Carmen and her ex-husband, Jeff, had been on-again, off-again. The night before she'd written this, she told me that Jeff had spent the night

Footsteps in the Attic

Photo by Paul F. Eno

The psychic tries to communicate with "Frank" by the east wall of the upstairs bedroom. The wall was completely white, but at right there appears to be a translucent object and other indications of a parallel reality.

with her. Carmen claimed that she'd been very aware of the entity's jealous presence. Carmen and Jeff had, of course, been intimate, and in the heat of it, Carmen claimed she had cried, "I died for you!"

Jeff said he too had felt the entity and had "freaked."

During November, Carmen announced that her card reader would come to the house the following evening and invited me to meet her. I arrived at about 9 p.m., took a quick turn around the yard to see if the electrical field there was as strong as ever (it was), and entered the house.

The card reader, whose name was Keri, wasn't in the living room as I'd expected. She was upstairs in the child's room trying to contact the entity! I flew upstairs to find a young woman with black hair, her hand against the room's east wall. She was very nice, but informed me that she was going to talk with the ghost, whose name was Frank!

I sat at the other end of the room in disgust as the well intentioned woman asked inane questions, such as, "What's it like over there? I'd really like to know! Rap once for 'yes,' twice for 'no'!"

Keri certainly was energized. At one point I watched what appeared to be a bolt of electricity or plasma shoot from her leg as she was in contact with "Frank's" wall.

Finally, Keri, who hadn't received a single answer, urged "Frank" to "give Carmen her space," and she finally got a rather angry rap "yes."

Even if my quantum interpretation of these phenomena is all wet, Keri's approach seemed rather air-headed to me. If this really was a human ghost, its mind would have been formed in some previous time, possibly even another century. How was it supposed to know what "give Carmen her space" meant, not to mention the other "I'm okay, you're okay" babble?

In any case, Carmen told me over the next few weeks that Keri's well-meaning efforts hadn't done any good. Surprise.

Then, on Christmas Eve, Jane's ex-husband, Bill, spent the night, sleeping on the living-room couch. He reported waking up in the wee hours to see an "older-looking" man in the adjacent kitchen. Interestingly, Bill reported that the refrigerator was "gone." I never found out for sure if this was Bill's sleepy imagination, dear old "Frank" or just a random time displacement possible at such a charged site. The absence of the refrigerator is a clue that it probably was a space-time slip and a "ghost from elsewhen."

In any case, my message to Carmen at that point was: "Time to take control and stop being a victim." Because of her personal struggles, however, she wasn't quite able to get a grip on this. Finally, for her own sake and that of Jane and her family, I did something I rarely do. Knowing that the entity was tied to the site, I urged Carmen to move. And, lo and behold, she took my advice. After a few weeks, she dug in at a much healthier house elsewhere in Burrillville.

Things immediately got better for Carmen. Her personal problems continued, but she got a job and began to put her failed marriage behind her. I was especially pleased to hear that she had no more paranormal trouble. Some months later, Carmen told me that she was going to marry a Native American elder she knew. I talked to her in 2002, even as I was finishing this book, and I'm happy to report that all is still well.

One point I hope to make here is that women don't have to put up with domination by parasites any more than they have to put up with it by abusive men. If you can't take control with your own positive power, pull up stakes and get a new start elsewhere. Refuse to be a victim, just as Carmen finally did!

In the Dark

The worst of it began when Helen Gadreau and David Lane simply tossed aside an old table that was taking up space in their basement. The one-story, duplex house in Burrillville, Rhode Island, had been a little strange for years, but the table incident marked the start of some real paranormal trouble. By the time a friend of theirs heard me lecture, then urged them to call me, Helen and Dave thought they were going crazy.

It was the night of November 1, 1998, and I picked my way along a dark side road in this rural, northern Rhode Island town on the Massachusetts border. When I finally found the house, on a rise set back from the road, I also found a very pleasant family group. Helen was in her early thirties, and Dave was about ten years older. They lived with Helen's lively children, nine year-old John and seven year-old Katie, in the house's larger section. In the smaller apartment lived Helen's friendly mother and step-father, Art and Sue Major, both in their early sixties. Even the dog seemed well adjusted.

But as the cliché goes, all wasn't as it appeared to be.

In taking my preliminary tour indoors, neither me, my camera nor my little electromagnetic-field meter picked up much of anything. I did feel something in a corner of young John's room, but it wasn't very strong. Could well have been a VLF sound phenomenon (see glossary and the introduction to the book).

The same held for the Majors' apartment. Nothing unusual that I could pick up.

Then I stepped through a small mud room and out into the pitch-black backyard. Wow! I was immediately awash in an electrical field so powerful that I nearly lost my footing. Something was watching me: I was as certain of that as if we'd been standing face to face. I headed down into the yard toward what seemed to be the center of the

Photo by Paul F. Eno

The author believes this was the primary parasite in the Gadreau case. It was the second time he had seen it. Household members saw it both in the yard and in the house. The white object in the background is part of a camping trailer. A photo expert suggested that the electrical field around the entity may have caused the digital photo to be out of focus.

electrical field.

I saw it with jolting suddenness, only about ten feet away. It was tall, glowing and shimmery, like a figure made of plasma. There was only a thin, whitish blankness where a face ought to have been, but I could clearly see its arms. I'm not afraid of these things, and they know it. As I continued to approach, the entity bolted to the right and vanished into the blackness. I chased it for a moment, but where or when it had gone, I obviously couldn't follow. The whole experience lasted about four seconds.

To have such a vivid encounter with the culprit, or one of them, right off the bat like this is unusual. On the rare occasions that I've actually seen parasites, they looked exactly like what I had just met. And it tipped me off to one thing: Whatever else was going on here, at least one of these miserable beasts was lined up at the buffet table at the expense of this family. My only regret so far was that I hadn't been quicker with my camera! But I'd remedy that later in the case.

Back in the house, the children were packed off to bed, and the grownups gathered around the table to tell me their story. It was a long one.

During the family's many years in the house, I was told, there sometimes had been feelings of presences, and there was the occasional out-of-place footstep or other sound. But whatever it was didn't seem overly intrusive. Most of the experiences always had happened to Helen.

"Then we moved that table earlier this year, and things went crazy!" Dave said. "We were just trying to clean out the basement!"

Every adult in the family now reported hearing footsteps from time to time when alone in the house. Thinking that another family member had come home, the hearer would go to look and usually find no-one there. Dave often heard female voices, sometimes calling his name. Often he would be convinced it was Helen's voice. The Majors showed me a kitchen cabinet that sometimes would rapidly open and close on its own. Mr. Major even reported being "tucked into bed" by something while he was alone at home one night.

Everyone reported the feeling of being watched through the windows by something outside the house. But it was the child-like Helen who endured the most even now. She felt vivid temperature changes, numerous presences, and had seen the apparition of a small blonde-haired girl, with flowers in her hair yet, in the master bedroom and hallway.

Helen and Dave were keeping the children in the dark about the whole thing, something I don't agree with. Children aren't stupid, and they tend to be very sensitive to these phenomena. Better to be forthright, reassur-

Footsteps in the Attic

The author uses his gauss meter on the infamous table.

ing and supportive. In any case, John and Katie were starting to report that they, too, were afraid.

How could a table make so much trouble? Well, I'm not so sure it did. As the Gadreau case developed, I tended to think that phenomena picking up after the table moved was just a coincidence. What we were dealing with here was one very strong parasite, a few lesser ones and the odd space-time slip. I had a hunch that the apparition of the little girl was no such slip, however, but the parasite trying to sew confusion and false assurances of security. After all, what could be more non-threatening than a little kid with flowers in her hair?

As I listened to their story that first night, I quickly saw that every adult in this family could be labeled "psychic" to one degree or another, but Helen considered herself quite psychic, and I believe she was right: She didn't miss much, seen or unseen, and hadn't throughout her life. In response to my standard question about occult activities, I found that she had read Tarot cards in the house. But Helen and everyone else denied using Ouija boards or doing séances.

Attitudes among these four people were strikingly different and very interesting. Helen, who came across as refreshingly innocent, was terrified, plain and simple. Dave was protective, afraid only for Helen. The Majors, to my surprise and alarm, thought the whole thing was rather neat. My whole approach just whizzed right by them. As the case developed – and worsened – the Majors actually expressed sympathy for the ghosts. Mrs. Major once referred to them as "cute"!

Give me a break!

Before I left that first night, I urged the family to "keep it positive" and try to build on their unity. As it turned out, this would be a big problem because there was a serious split between Helen and her parents over Dave, a split that I soon came to realize had more to do with the worsening paranormal situation than any table did.

This case escalated rapidly. After Christmas I returned to the house with Joe Frisella, the soil engineer, who pointed out that the whole lot, well over an acre, was mostly fill and may or may not have been overly electrical. We did note, though, that high-tension wires ran past the north of the property. They were several hundred yards away, but the land between them and the back of the Gadreau house seemed low and wet – an electromagnetic stage that could well lead to some paranormal drama.

That's why I wasn't surprised when a neighbor reported having seen a "UFO" on the property the previous year – yet another electromagnetic phenomenon, in all probability.

It was now 1999, and January wasn't very old when I got a call from Helen. She and Dave had started to see shadowy figures "about the size of children."

"It was only last night," Helen told me. "I was in the kitchen, and I actually heard the floor creak. I turned around, and one of those little shadow figures was behind me. When I turned around, it took off into Katie's room!"

The previous week, she said she had seen another small, shadowy apparition go into John's room and literally pick up a pair of jeans.

Footsteps in the Attic

"I thought it was John, but he was asleep in the bed!" she told me.

A few nights later I was back, with Joe Frisella and, wonder of wonders, my wife, Jackie. My better half is very psychic, but she's not comfortable with it. In nearly twenty years of marriage, this was the first time she had ever accompanied me on a case! I got her to come along because she has wonderful "people skills," and I thought she could help perk up Helen, who obviously was the parasites' main focus.

The more Jackie and I spoke with Helen, the clearer it became that this guileless young lady was the perfect target. She was vulnerable, dependent and had been at the blunt end of the stick for most of her life. Among other mishaps, Helen, when a child, had discovered the body of a murdered friend. Later, there had been family problems and an abusive marriage. She had reached something of a plateau now, and, to all appearances, Dave and the children were the lights of her life.

Ironically and sadly, Dave continued to be the focus of tension between Helen and her parents. From what I could see, this was because he and Helen weren't married and because Dave, who was going to school in preparation for a career change, wasn't working steadily. The chemistry here wasn't good, and the parasites were the only ones benefiting from it.

Helen stated that she often felt "something on me." She said she didn't sleep well because of the shadowy apparitions. I didn't disbelieve her. There were too many other witnesses, including me. But I couldn't ignore the impression that she enjoyed being the center of so much attention, something quite common in parasite, especially poltergeist, cases. So I was on high alert for signs of embellishment.

At the same time, Helen never seemed to develop one of those wildly unhealthy bonds with a parasite, such as

Footsteps in the Attic

I was seeing in the Carmen Kerrigan case that had begun only a few months before.

Meanwhile, this was the night I was going to capture one of the best paranormal photos of my long career: None other than boss parasite, my acquaintance from that first night in the backyard!

I was out there again because Dave had reported walking the dog one night and hearing footsteps coming up behind him. He had turned around but could see no-one. I was walking slowly through the same part of the yard, and I suddenly felt that strong electrical field wash over me. When there was a flash right in front of me, my digital camera was ready.

I don't trust flash photos taken at night. Backflashes that look like orbs or other phenomena can bounce back from anything shiny, even bugs in the air. So whenever possible I go back to the same spot in daylight to see if any object there could have created the illusion of an anomaly. Back in the Gadreau yard the next afternoon, I found an old tomato-plant stake in the ground that might have reflected. But later measurements indicated that the stake would have been well out of the camera's field of vision. It was much shorter than the object in the picture, and it certainly didn't have arms or create electrical fields!

On the last evening in January, I was back at the house, listening to Helen describe more shadow apparitions. Dave reported seeing the same glowing figure I'd seen, both in the house and in the yard after dark. He also said there had been a glowing orb and what looked like white, shiny "eyes." Then, Helen had seen the "streak" figure in the bedroom and, later, a black, dog-like figure, possibly a tulpa (see glossary and the introduction to the book).

Meanwhile, the Majors declared that they had awakened on a recent night to a shaking bed and a "weight," as though something were sitting on their legs. So much for cute ghosts.

Footsteps in the Attic

In a particularly nasty turn of events, Dave showed me some bruises he said had appeared on his body while he slept. I'd seen this happen in other cases: Yes, parasites can be jealous!

As if that weren't enough, everyone recalled that something had started pounding on the walls just after Christmas. It had happened only once, but I saw it as "only the beginning" of a serious poltergeist outbreak unless something was done at once. Of course, some of these incidents may have had mundane explanations. But I wasn't taking any chances. It was time to act.

The first step was to get Helen's permission to have a long talk with the children, who were as jumpy as hens by this time. I told John and Katie that they had nothing to be afraid of, and I explained as best I could what was going on. I stressed that what mattered was sticking together as a family, loving each other and trusting God. I promised to do everything I could to help, and I gave them each an Eastern Orthodox icon of the guardian angel. Helen and Dave already had been taking time each night to pray and read the Bible with the children.

Actually, the family wasn't connected with a church, but there was some Roman Catholic background. So I brought holy water and a medal of the Blessed Virgin Mary. Used properly, both of these "sacramentals" can evoke powerful positive energy. I always have found holy water especially useful when used with faith. All water is holy, as are all the good things of the multiverse. But water that has been concentrated upon and prayed over by people filled with faith and love can perfect the holiness that's already there. Just as parasites may draw power from wet, electromagnetic ground, so they can be pushed back by water shot through with positive power and, I stress again, used with faith.

Dave, Helen and I went from room to room, and I had Helen sprinkle holy water in each. I meant this to be an empowering experience for her, and by this time I was explaining to her again and again that she had to take control of the situation: No more a victim!

All went well until we got into the basement, where I could feel a great deal of energy in and near the furnace room. Dave and I suddenly looked at Helen. She had stopped, her eyes were blank and some of her hair was standing up. She wasn't putting this on.

"I feel it on me!" she said, her voice nervous but not fearful. Then, suddenly: "He says you'll never find him."

"We've already found him," I replied calmly. Then, to it: "We know what you are, and you will leave this woman alone. You have powers arrayed against you that you can't possibly imagine!"

"He's laughing!" she said. "But he doesn't want you here and he doesn't want the holy water."

"Enough!" I said. "Dave, take Helen's hand!"

I took one hand and Dave the other. Immediately, the thing backed off. I called upon God, Goddess, angels and every other positive power I could think of to help protect Helen, and to help build love and protection in this house! In another moment, the thing was gone. Helen looked and felt normal again.

It was because of this incident that the light bulb really went on for Dave.

"After we did that, I can really see what you mean about love driving this thing out!" he said.

It was true. All my preaching to Dave and Helen couldn't have gotten my point across any better than this experience with that rotten little parasite. The fact that it backed right off when we held Helen's hands in a simple act of love and solidarity taught the lesson best!

But I got an interesting reaction from Helen when I gave her advice that I frequently give to parasite victims: Call upon your loving ancestors to help.

"I don't want any more ghosts!" she said.

Footsteps in the Attic

I'd never heard it put this way before.

"These aren't ghosts, they're your extended family and, no matter where or when they are, they love you!"

It turned out that Helen had experienced a "visitation apparition" (see Part 4) from a beloved aunt right after the lady had passed on. It's very rare to be afraid of such visits from loved ones, but Helen was so gun shy about the paranormal by then that she had been scared silly. According to Helen, the aunt just wanted to tell her she was alright, apologized for startling her, and was never heard from again!

After the incident in the basement, though, Helen got steadily stronger. Dave seemed to be her rock. By March, Helen's increased self-confidence and power was keeping the parasite at bay – at least for her. There were indications that the main parasite had given up on her and was trying to go after Katie, but the family was supporting the child, too.

Helen and Dave reported that the entity would get frustrated now that it couldn't get at Helen. They would hear it literally pacing up and down in the hallway! Phenomena like this continued, though to a lesser degree, and the shadow figures faded away. The Majors, still doubtful about my theories, weren't participating in our remedies and became increasingly out of touch with the situation. The tension between the two sides of the house went on, which made beating this all the more difficult. Still, the path toward a poltergeist outbreak seemed to have been blocked. But some closure was needed.

On March 21, I was at the house with one of my photography experts, Eric Baillargeon, probably the only member of my team more skeptical than I was! Eric was there to photograph what I call the "bell and candle ceremony," a generic, family-oriented prayer of protection that I made up. It's not an exorcism, and it's very simple.

I carried a candle, and we all went from room to room.

Dave and the author hold Helen's hand as she blanks out during a house-cleansing effort.

At each door and window, I would make the figure-eight sign, which represents infinity, and say words to the effect that, "May all that is holy, good, right and true come into this house and into the hearts of all who live here. And may all evil flee!"

When there are children, as in this case, I have them go ahead of us into each room ringing a little guardian-angel wind chime, which always makes them smile and gives them confidence. The bell or chime is one very ancient method for "purifying" the energy in a room. John and Katie also carried the angel icons I'd given them earlier.

At one point, in the first-floor hallway, Helen seemed to black out for a moment. Dave and I had to support her, and she quickly recovered. She couldn't pin down quite what had happened. Perhaps her old nemesis had made another vain attempt to come through. Still, I later advised Dave to keep track of any future incidents like this for possible medical attention.

This stopped the trouble, at least for awhile. For much of the rest of 1999, I was pleased to hear that things were fine at *Maison Gadreau*. The entities, which I knew by then were attached to the land, always were in the background but were well under control. With critters of that kind, that's about as good a result as I can expect if the person or people who have "connected" are going to stay at the site.

In October, however, the family was having more trouble. Evidently, the entity was making another try for Katie. But Dave and Helen had learned a great deal about keeping things positive, and they knew what to do. I didn't even have to get involved.

I talked with Helen again in March 2000. Things were great with her and, she said, aside from the occasional outdoor sighting, all was well.

Drawn by Murder

It was a frustrating Sunday evening, and it marked the beginning of one of my most frustrating cases.

I had just showered and was looking forward to a comfortable evening vegetating with my wife and our sons. I was just settling down in the family room when the phone rang, and I had to dress and leave the house on an errand I'd forgotten. I had just donned the pajamas and robe a second time when the phone rang again.

"The cops told me to call you," said a thin, slightly gravelly voice.

Was this Edward G. Robinson?

"I got real trouble with a ghost here! Can you come down?"

After a sigh and a few questions, I found out that I was listening to Roger Therrien, a middle-aged man with serious health problems who lived only about a half-mile from me in Woonsocket, Rhode Island. He claimed that the police had come to his four-unit apartment house that evening on a noise complaint by a neighbor. Outside, he said, they'd heard a racket coming from inside. Once inside, they'd heard and found nothing. This happened several times.

According to Roger, one of the officers had gone back to his cruiser and refused to come out. The ranking cop, he added, had told him to call me and even gave him my phone number. I was never able to fully corroborate this story with the Woonsocket police, but the chief did invite me to donate a copy of *Faces at the Window* for the department's training room. Indeed, police, clergy and psychiatrists are the professionals most likely to run into paranormal phenomena when victims first seek help.

Anyway, Roger complained that he and his fellow tenants were being vigorously harassed by a ghost, had seen minor poltergeist activity, were creeped out by feelings of presences, heard strange sounds and saw the occasional apparition.

I took pity, got dressed again and headed out into this chilly December 1998 night.

Driving down the hill and across the railroad tracks to an area that was in the midst of an "urban renewal" project, I parked in front of the boxy house to which Roger had directed me. My first encounter was with his spastic little poodle, which kept barking at the seemingly empty hallway and at certain corners. The poor thing looked completely bedraggled, and its blood pressure must have been sky high. Later in the case, it was to die of a heart attack.

Inside one of the two first-floor apartments I found Roger, a thin, friendly man with glasses, and his quiet, grey-haired companion, Jan. Both were in their mid-fifties and were absolute sweethearts. Their apartment was tiny, and I had trouble getting Roger to hold off with his story until I'd had a chance to look around. I moved about

Photo by Paul F. Eno

During the author's first visit to the Therrien case site, energy seems to pour from the windows of a vacant apartment, and the windows reflect a sunset that took place five hours earlier.

Footsteps in the Attic

Photo by Paul F. Eno
The intriguing cellar door at the back of the apartment house. To the naked eye, the wall was completely clean, but in the photo, streaks, grime and shadows seem to appear as energy again hovers around the windows.

the place, snapped some pictures, then followed Roger upstairs to a second apartment he rented for storage purposes. I got a general negative impression throughout the house, but nothing definite. Something – lots of things — had gone on here, but I couldn't quite put my finger on specifics.

No sooner had we plopped into chairs back at Roger's than there was an indefinite sound across the hallway in the other first-floor apartment, which had been dark when I arrived. Roger's dog started yipping again, lights came on under the neighbor's door, and a television started blathering.

"She (the neighbor) said she saw a ghost come out of her bedroom wall. She was scared silly and just left," Roger explained in a nervous voice. "Maybe she came back."

Footsteps in the Attic

128

We both rapped on the door. No answer.

"Maybe she has her TV and lights on timers," I suggested, realizing that wasn't likely since everything in the apartment seemed to be on.

The next thing I learned was that this was to be one of my most, shall we say, photogenic cases. Anomalies appeared in roughly forty percent of photos taken at the site, an amazing number. The first batch came from my outside circuit of the building that first night. In several, one can see the energy just pouring out of the windows and doors! Indoor shots show many ball-lightning-like orbs, so familiar in today's paranormal photography.

I was especially riveted by the basement door at the back of the building. Not only did anomalies appear in photos of it, but I was convinced that there was something extremely interesting behind it. Roger, unfortunately, had no key to the basement, something he would remedy in a unique way later.

It turned out that Jan had lived in the apartment for

Photo by Shane Sirois
Orbs at the right seem to be checking out investigator John LaRochelle in the basement during the Therrien case.

Footsteps in the Attic

Residents claimed that this money spontaneously appeared on their bed.
Photo by Paul F. Eno

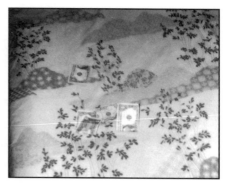

about sixteen years, and Roger had moved in some ten years after that. Things always had been a little weird in the house, Jan said, but gradually started to pick up after Roger moved in. It worsened after he became disabled and was stuck in the apartment day in and day out. Roger had ailments that would fill a medical text. With very little income, he and Jan saw no immediate prospect of moving.

A Roman Catholic, Roger nonetheless believed that he and Jan were very psychic, and he offered a long list of his life experiences in evidence, including "prophetic" dreams and telepathic experiences. At the same time, Roger and Jan both swore that they hadn't been involved in occult practices, such as Ouija boards and séances, that would have drawn parasites.

Along with the apparitions and other phenomena, Roger described something that most of my case subjects wouldn't have complained about: the spontaneous appearance of money! I never saw this happen, but Roger and Jan both swore that dollar bills and sometimes loose change would just appear on their bed.

"I'd never believe it if you told me, but we keep finding money on our bed, over $90 so far. We don't dare spend it; we just keep it in a drawer!" he told me.

As if that weren't enough, Roger and Jan said they would hear each other's voices saying some very negative things – even when the other wasn't home. That's

Footsteps in the Attic

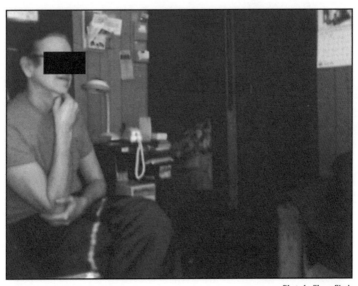

Photo by Shane Sirois

Roger Therrien sits in his living room as an eerie band of light wraps around his leg.

also common in parasite cases, and really sets off the alarm bells for me.

I dread cases in apartment buildings. I almost never can talk with all the tenants, and the management people usually think I'm a nut, not to mention a potential pub-lic-relations nightmare. With all the different kinds of people living in such places, who knows what goes on – or what's going on there in other parts of the multiverse? As the Therrien case began, Roger and Jan were the only tenants left in the house. The apartment above them was vacant, as was the extra one Roger rented. The first-floor neighbor, according to Roger, had run off into the blue. I never even met her.

After several visits and some fruitless attempts at re-searching the building's history, I concluded – largely from the photographs and my own impressions — that the place harbored both parasites and manifestations of "ghosts from elsewhen." I felt all sorts of presences, male

Footsteps in the Attic

and female. That's not especially unusual at such energized sites, but the main problem in this case has been Roger: He evidently made a world-class connection with the house's parasites.

Working with middle-aged to older parasite victims can be very difficult because of the black-and-white worldview most of them grew up with. Mention to a younger person that the answer to their problem is bringing in positive energy to displace the negative energy and they usually have a nodding acquaintance with what you're talking about. Older people often have trouble understanding that: They expect people like me simply to "come in and fix it."

For people with loyalties to a church, like Roger and Jan, I consult their clergy whenever possible because their prayers and blessings can be vital tools. Used with love, they can help stir victims' faith and confidence to take control of a hostile situation.

Photo by Shane Sirois
A figure seems to flow from the left wall of the bedroom in the Therrien apartment.

Footsteps in the Attic

Roger mentioned that he had gone to his priest for help, but the good cleric had, not surprisingly, little knowledge about how to deal with such things. He had put Roger in touch with a priest in nearby Pawtucket, who sounded to me like the exorcist for the Diocese of Providence. Every Roman Catholic diocese has, or is supposed to have, at least one priest who is educated about the paranormal (or the church's narrow vision of it), fills the bill as investigator and, if necessary, exorcist. This is all extremely hush-hush, of course, and understandably so.

As a Roman Catholic seminary student many years ago, I had the honor of studying under two of the best paranormal experts (and very prayerful men) in the American Catholic Church of the day, the Jesuit priest John J. Nicola and Fr. Lawrence Cotter of the Diocese of Ogdensburg, New York. But I haven't met their like in many a year and hope they aren't extinct!

Today, dealing with most Roman Catholic priests is a pain in the neck for me. Few of them know anything about the paranormal and, when they hear about my theories, which don't necessarily mesh with church doctrine, they tend to be hostile, indifferent or confused. The priest I met with in Pawtucket as Roger's case got under way struck me as sincere but insufferably narrow. My ideas apparently went over his head.

"I don't believe in ghosts. I believe in demons," he pronounced.

To my surprise, he knew all about Roger and Jan, recognized that they had a paranormal problem but couldn't get by the fact that they lived together without being married.

"They have to straighten out their spiritual lives before I can help them," he said.

I'm no bleeding-heart liberal. I believe that manners and morals make life better for everyone, especially children. Society's rules (what's left of them) have developed over millennia and are there so that human interaction doesn't degenerate into chaos. And bravo to straightening out our spiritual lives: Assuming that the spirituality is constructive, it's the best way to start bringing in positive energy and power.

Roger and Jan struck me as without guile, completely oblivious to the priest's implied claim that they were so steeped in sin that the "demon" couldn't be banished. They were asking for help from their own church, and its representative was refusing to meet them halfway with the compassion necessary for spiritual repairs to begin. At least keep in touch with these people, bless their house and visit once in awhile! That keeps channels open. Hurling down moral thunderbolts from on high rarely accomplishes anything.

Needless to say, the priest was no help.

Meanwhile, Roger had become an online pen pal with Silent Bear, a Blackfoot elder from New Hampshire. While I've met some Native American elders who have ideas just as preconceived as priests, I find most of them to be sober, spiritually mature, compassionate and very sensitive to what's going on in my cases. So when Roger said that Silent Bear was coming to Woonsocket one Saturday a few months after my investigation began, I had few qualms.

I was more right than I knew.

Silent Bear, otherwise known as Shane Sirois, turned out to be a young, capable, sensitive family man and to have all the qualities I've seen in the best paranormal investigators. I'm a very solitary person and don't get close to people easily, but Shane and I were brothers from the start. Of course, it didn't hurt when I mentioned space-time slips and parasites and he knew exactly what I was talking about! Shane gave Roger the same advice I did about bringing in positive energy to displace the negative.

Footsteps in the Attic

"Well, if you both say it, I guess I should try and do it," he quipped. That would turn out to be very difficult for Roger because of his weak physical condition.

A few weekends later, Shane appeared in Woonsocket once again, this time with paranormal researcher John LaRochelle of Massachusetts, who also was to become a good friend. The three of us went to see Roger, and it was to be an interesting day: We got into the basement.

"It dawned on me that all I had to do was take the bolts out of the hinges!" Roger said.

The basement actually was quite modern and rather clean, but I could see that some of its stone walls dated back at least to the early 1900s. There was some evidence of a fire in an original structure and that the place had been rebuilt.

Shane had an infrared video camera, and it got a workout in that basement. The place was filled with orbs, some of which could be seen with the naked eye. On one occasion, my still camera caught an orb racing across the basement, while Shane got the same orb on video.

While they can be solid clues that paranormal condi-

Photo by Paul F. Eno
An orb streaks across the basement from left to right. Shane Sirois captured the same orb on videotape.

Footsteps in the Attic

tions exist, I'm still undecided as to exactly what orbs are. Dust, lens effects, geomagnetic phenomena, ball lightning, light angles, electrical fields, light leaks (if you're using film) or defects in digital cameras or standard film all can cause orbs or other gadgets people will point to excitedly as paranormal. When we see orbs with the naked eye, often they're just static electricity firing off in our optic nerves.

I certainly can testify that there are orbs for which I can see no explanation but a paranormal one. Heck, I've seen them often enough with the naked eye when investigating cases both indoors and outdoors. I've seen them in several different colors. I've been followed by them, and I've seen them manifest what I can only interpret as consciousness and even intelligence.

When all other possibilities are exhausted, I think that orbs could be entities from other parts of space-time or at least electrical manifestations of their presence. I'm also open to the theory that orbs may be plasma- or electrically-based life forms of a kind all their own, existing in our own part of the multiverse, almost like the "skyfish" I discuss in the introduction to this book.

What really interests me is that orbs seem much more common than they used to be. When I'd take case photos twenty-five or thirty years ago, I'd rarely notice orbs. While they'd show up in troubled homes now and then, they didn't seem to be a major phenomenon. Today, they're all over the place. Perhaps modern film and photographic equipment are more apt to pick up their light spectra.

No matter what orbs may be, however, Roger's apartment house was alive with them on some days. It wasn't long before I brought in some of my investigatory gang: soil engineer Joe Frisella, historian Wendy Reardon and, of course, Shane and John. It was the second trip into the basement. Wendy, who also is an expert in the literature of death and dying, brought my attention to the corner of the basement just under Roger's apartment.

"My right ear hurts when I stand here," she pointed out.

So did mine, and so did almost everyone else's. I also got a headache, and I never get headaches! A thorough check revealed no evidence of machinery or electronic devices that could have caused such a reaction. Our only conclusion was that we were picking up and empathizing with a terrible event taking place on this spot somewhere in space-time.

We believed that a woman had been killed – or would be killed — in this corner of the basement, perhaps accidentally. Such a traumatic event always sends out significant ripples through the multiverse, and in such an electromagnetically charged place as this, those ripples must be tremendous.

I recalled that Woonsocket had been a crowded, rough-and-tumble mill town, a sort of New England Dodge City, well into the twentieth century. A murder or fatal accident could well be taking place in those times and no-one would be the wiser. Not to sound melodramatic, but it wouldn't surprise me at all if the body were buried in that basement. With its new concrete floor, however, it would take more money than I have to find out. Not only would such a terrible event be evident to anyone sensitive enough to pick it up, but it could attract parasites that would be delighted to find an emotional and physical "sitting duck" like Roger.

This scenario was bad enough without the various and sundry other paranormal bric-a-brac going on in this place. I advised Roger and Jan to move, but they assured me they had neither the money nor the inclination to do so.

In ensuing months, we did everything we could to turn Roger into a positive thinker, to disconnect him from the parasites. We would visit, as would his brother, a positive fellow who also lived in Woonsocket. We deliberately engaged Roger in lively conversations, made him laugh, and urged him to get involved in outside activities. Whenever we did this, phenomena would die down or disappear, often for weeks.

Roger did take our advice as well as he could, even plunging into a successful campaign to save a historic local church that had been destined for the wrecking ball. And by late 2000, we seemed to have made significant progress – for Roger.

"They've (the parasites) been leaving me alone, but now they're after Jan!"

Jan, also in a weakened physical condition by then, has had a difficult time and has been an off-and-on parasite target since. In early 2001, Roger learned that he had cancer serious enough to endanger his life. That didn't help the positive thinking.

As I write this, Roger and Jan continue to struggle, both with their unwelcome guests and with illness. A Hispanic family has moved into the vacant upstairs apartment, but I haven't yet spoken with them. At this point, moving still is Roger's and Jan's best hope for disentanglement. Roger, who seems to be beating the cancer so far, assured me for the first time since this started that he and Jan really are going to try to move.

I hope they do so: They're great folks and don't deserve what they've received at the hands of these cosmic criminals. And I might add that we all need the rest!

Footsteps in the Attic

4

THE ANCESTORS

Take heart! Indifferent "ghosts from elsewhen" and nasty parasites aren't the only entities we share quantum reality with. I'm convinced that there are far more of what we would consider good entities scattered across space-time than there are bad ones. I'm sure that most either have limited access to other parts of the multiverse (as is the case with us) or have better things to do than get involved with the likes of us.

But there are some who seem to be located and motivated to actually help us. Just as parasites are the origin of concepts such as demons and vampires, I'm sure that positive entities are responsible for our experiences of angels, guardian spirits, beneficial nature spirits and other good entities. And in their own worlds they're probably just as physical as we are.

Deathless love: Honoring our ancestors

On a personal level, I'm convinced that these positive entities include some of our ancestors who, if our vision of quantum reality is correct, are always alive somewhere or somewhen and, from what I've seen, can be vividly connected with those of their own blood throughout space-time.

When I urge parasite victims to call upon their good ancestors for help, most people of Western Hemisphere descent have little or no idea what I'm talking about, and I have to explain until the cows come home. For most of us, interest in our blood forbears, especially distant ones, is limited to where they fit in our family tree and whether they were famous. Except for one or two generations back, thinking of them as family simply doesn't occur to most of us. And to actively love our ancestors, pray for them and have a certainty that they are by our sides in one form or another is an alien idea.

People of oriental descent, however, know exactly what I mean, since honoring the ancestors is an important part of many Eastern Hemisphere religions and cultures.

Regardless of their own cultural beliefs, many people I've worked with over the years have been astounded at how "adopting" and learning to love their ancestors as family members has changed their lives and attitudes. And when it comes to fighting off parasites, I've seen ancestors come to the rescue time and again. They are truly powerful allies!

I should qualify this by saying that all of us have a few ancestors who are jerks, at least in our corner of space-time. But I find that our feelings tend to be drawn not to them but to those who are most aware of us and are most in a position to help. I explain how all this might work in Part 5.

This isn't some corny, New Age, feel-good idea. It's quantum mechanics at its personal best.

Every family has its stories of members who have appeared to loved ones at times of death or crisis to warn or reassure. Paranormal investigators usually refer to these as visitation apparitions. Over the years I've heard a mountain of these stories. Occasionally they turn out to be parasites mimicking recently passed relatives, but loved ones tend to see through this sooner or later. The real visitation apparition is so positive ninety-nine percent of the time that I've yet to have one turn into a case.

Buddha was right

Gautama the Buddha, whom Dr. C.S. Shah calls "the sanest man the world has ever seen," taught that we must have compassion for all things. "Truth and Knowledge flowed from his every pore as Compassion, in his austerities and tapas, kindness and humility, and suffering and feelings."

I couldn't agree more with that exhortation. My rule is, pray for everything and everyone, all the time. Ancestors, friends, enemies, people you don't know, animals you don't know, the Earth…the universes. If you've suffered a miscarriage or had an abortion, pray for your unborn child: He or she is very much alive somewhere or somewhen and loves you – no matter what.

Praying and "saying prayers" are two very different things. Prayer is a state of being. If you try to live it, you'll learn what I mean: Prayer is the greatest act of love there is, and love is the greatest power in the multiverse.

Angels and guardian spirits

I'm surprised when I find anyone who doesn't have some story of a lucky coincidence or a miraculous escape. People who don't are pretty rare. To all "primitive" cultures, of course, encounters with angels, guardian spirits, positive nature spirits or what have you are normal. These presumably non-human entities seem to be in parallel universes with easy access to us, and many appear to have the best quality we know of in living beings: an utterly selfless desire to help others.

A warning

Many people tell me they're convinced that Aunt Ruth is watching over them because every time they go out for the evening, she does the laundry. Don't laugh, I've actually heard this!

Be careful! Ancestors and guardian spirits will come across as warm, gentle, unobtrusive and loving presences. Don't try to actively communicate with them. You don't need to. Sure, I meet people who talk to their ancestors or guardians. But I think our lives are full of too many words as it is. Best to commune in silence.

As the ancients knew, respect is the operative word. In my daily rule of prayer at home, I thank "all good and gracious spirits of this place" for their hospitality and protection, adding "may you always be honored by those who live here." I also remember all my ancestors and loved ones, asking for the prayers of those in a position to offer them and praying for those who aren't.

When entering the woods or fields I love so well, I always touch the Earth and ask the guardians' permission "to enter with love and respect."

But if any entity starts intruding into your life, chances are you're not dealing with anything positive. Let your heart and your common sense – not your imagination or your wishful thinking – be your guide!

The Grassless Grave

As I hope I've shown in this book, quantum reality is a two-way street. Just as our ancestors can help us, we can help them.

After a book signing in New Hampshire in 1999, a woman came up to me and asked why no grass would grow on her grandfather's grave. The man had died in 1962. I asked a few questions about him, and was told that he had a pitiful life, was horrendously unhappy and had the personality of a cactus.

"Love him and pray for him with all your might," I told the woman, who had been afraid of grandpa in life but was sorry for him now.

Apparently, the woman really took me seriously. She mobilized her family, had prayer services at the graveside, and dug out old pictures of grandpa and put them in places of honor. Six months later, I received a happy e-mail saying that the man's grave was now lush with grass. As a matter of fact, the cemetery caretakers had to cut the plot twice a week that summer!

The White Sword

One of the most inspiring examples I've seen of ancestral aid was in 1988, during a brief but most unpleasant poltergeist case in Portland, Maine. A mean little parasite was harassing a family of four, concentrating on the teenaged daughter. All my attempts to get her to bring in positive energy got nowhere because she was so completely petrified.

So why not have someone else bring in positive energy? In a conference with the parents, I asked if there was an ancestor the girl had been attached to. The usual answer I get is, "Sure, Great Grandma Sue or Grandpa Joe."

Not this time.

"Well," replied dad, scratching his chin, "She really relates to this guy Henry Walke, who fought in the Civil War."

It turned out that Walke, a Union naval officer prominent during some of the campaigns on the Mississippi River, was one of the girl's maternal great-great-great grandparents. According to mom, he had ended up an admiral, had died in 1896 and had a destroyer named after him. The girl was fascinated with his story and even had his picture in her room.

This was perfect!

When I suggested she ask for her ancestor's help, the girl gave me a blank look for a moment, then "came the dawn." She was intrigued, even excited. A week later, I received a frantic phone call from the family. The girl herself was in tears.

"It was the most wonderful thing I ever saw!" she cried.

As I had advised, the girl for several days projected love toward her great-great-great granddad and had asked for his protection against the parasite. She even had slept with Walke's picture under her pillow.

The night before she called me, the parasite had attacked, blowing things off shelves in the room and pulling the covers off her bed. The girl's screams brought the rest of the family just in time to feel what they described as "a warm breeze blowing through the room." Then – and all four said they saw this – what looked like a glowing white rod or sword flashed through the air in front of the girl's bed. There was thumping on the walls for a few seconds, the "sword" vanished and utter quiet descended.

Admiral Henry Walke, USN

The parasite was never heard from again.

The girl noted with some emotion that in his picture, Rear Admiral Henry Walke, USN, wears his officer's sword prominently at his side.

Footsteps in the Attic

5

DEATH: THE FINAL FRONTIER?

"O death, where is thy victory? O death, where is thy sting?"
1 Corinthians 15:55

Death: The ending of life. The entire premise of this book is that there is no such thing. Still, we cry as we watch our loved ones pass away. We bury strangers and friends alike. We watch the television news and see thousands perish.

Indeed, "the dead" loom like living monuments over all of us. We live in the nations they founded, in the communities they carved out, in homes they built. We obey laws they made and enjoy the freedom they bled for. We inherit their money. The art, music and literature they created still touch our hearts and stir our imaginations. We worship in ways they taught because that's the way they met God.

But bodily death is like money. We see notes and coins, but these are just symbols. Money has no objective reality. It, like time and death, are abstractions. They're all functions of our consciousness.

People aren't abstractions, however. You're here, body, mind and soul. What's more, your consciousness, your existence, reaches out across space-time in all sorts of facets and manifestations. But not only will you experience physical death, you're experiencing it right now in countless ways in unknowable numbers in unimagined universes. But not to worry: You're in plenty of other places elsewhere and elsewhen! There is no death because there is *never* an absence of life. You truly are made in the image of God because, in a very real way, you are eternal.

Where will I go when my body dies?

Whenever I hear that question, another pops into my head: Where were you before your body was conceived? I think the answer to both questions is the same: Where you already are.

A relative of mine who had terminal cancer asked me one day: "Paul, you're into this. What happens when we die?"

"Well," I replied, "Maybe *nothing* happens when we die. Maybe our consciousness just shifts our attention to where we already are in the easiest-to-reach parallel universe. Maybe we just wake up out of a sound sleep and say, 'Jeez! What a weird dream *that* was!"

This new awareness may be in what you would consider the past or the future. It might be in a completely alien world. Your body might be quite different there. But it's still you, and you still are connected with those you love, who also are sprinkled across space-time in myriad ways.

After getting to know ghosts for over thirty years, I'm convinced that this is very close to what becomes of us or, more accurately, *what the essence of our life really is.* I think these shifts of consciousness that we call death are the root experiences of our existence.

Of course, there are universes and universes. Down deep, our religions remember that. One dimension that our religions – and my own experience with angels and ancestors – point out is that we don't all "go" to the same "places."

If you're one of those rare people who already experience the cosmic vastness of your consciousness *by letting go of the here-and-now self,* you can become one of the truly great. Religions speak of "saints," "the chosen" or "the enlightened." Invariably, these are people whom love and compassion have taught to *already live outside of themselves.* They know that the sense of self is an illusion, so they embrace the multiverse, standing in the presence of God, the Being of ultimate compassion, humility, justice and selflessness. When bodily death occurs, I believe this draws their consciousnesses to universes in which they can most easily do what they already do best: love and help others, perhaps throughout space-time. These may include our most powerful helping ancestors and other spiritual guardians.

Ordinary people like you and me probably are drawn to universes similar to where we are now. If we have enough compassion, however, we or some part of us may rest in a universe where we have easier access to those we love elsewhere or elsewhen. From there, we may become loving ancestors.

Many religions talk about hell, not a popular idea in today's "I'm okay, you're okay" society. The myths of eternal fire descend from the ancient theological concept that the ultimate desolation – the ultimate pain — for anyone or anything is separation from God. I don't think this is so easy to do because we are *homo adorans*: worshipping man. For us, loving and striving for deity is as basic an instinct as eating, and anyone who denies it is a liar or a fool. There is no such thing as an atheist.

But for the worst of us, the unrepentant murderers, abusers and other predators, those who cling to and worship the self so ferociously that it destroys others and themselves, I believe consciousness is trapped in universes of endless aloneness. While I don't believe I've ever seen it, I'm open to the idea that they could be parasites, just as they are in our universe.

In a very, very real way, you make your own cosmic "bed" in the multiverse. In the popular mind, heaven is the place, usually "in the sky," where you've "made it," where you'll be eternally happy. But can we be eternally happy without change? With endless sameness, no matter how glorious?

The quantum vision offers both timelessness *and* eternal change, in perfect unity. Sounds pretty good to me, as long as our general direction is improvement!

Footsteps in the Attic

Reincarnation?

In what sometimes strikes me as a terminally adolescent society, losing the self -- which we equate with the body -- can be a nearly unbearable concept even though selfishness is our greatest source of frustration. The worst horror imaginable to the typical modern Westerner is dying and losing his or her precious self. That's not only why so many people have such a terror of bodily death, but also why they cling to a rather vague and childish concept of reincarnation.

None of what I describe here is reincarnation. There are no past lives in quantum reality because there is no time. These are parallel lives, lives we already are living, and they can be in what to us is either the past or the future.

Regression questions

I have a love-hate relationship with hypnotism. In paranormal research in the 1960s, it carried great weight, then lost credibility for many. Today, it's been rehabilitated in many circles and is relied upon by people like regression therapists, who hypnotize their subjects to take them back through "past lives." Regression therapists can range from reputable psychiatrists to self-appointed gurus with mail-order certificates. They believe that regression can help people confront problems they had in these other lives and that continue in the current one. I've seen cases in which this sort of therapy has been quite effective, especially in dealing with phobias.

If our ideas about quantum reality are correct, and assuming that hypnosis does what it appears to do, then what subjects see are parallel lives, and there ought to be reports of "future" lives as well as "past" ones.

There are.

For many years, I've made it a point to ask regression therapists if they ever encounter worlds they don't recognize. "Many times" or "funny you should ask" are common answers. Most hypnotists tell me that they ask their subjects what year it is when they describe a "past" life. They've had people say it's 2148, 2287, 3270 and combinations of numbers and even letters the therapists don't recognize.

I'm pleased to see that ideas of parallel lives are beginning to work their way into popular reincarnation theory. Maybe they're finally beginning to "get it."

What about NDEs?

Near-death experiences (NDEs) are all the rage today. With advances in medical technology, more and more people are being "brought back" from the edge of bodily death or from well beyond the edge. While a few report horrific experiences, most tell similar stories of a tunnel of light with loved ones, guardian spirits or deities waiting for them at the end. The NDE seems to be universal, cutting across all cultures and ethnicities.

Most of these experiences can be duplicated with electrodes under laboratory conditions, *but that doesn't mean they aren't real*. Some scientists say the NDE is completely illusory, the result of neurons firing wildly as the brain dies. They believe it's a product of the brain's evolution and nothing more. Well, products of evolution supposedly are there because of "natural selection." They have survival value. What's the survival value of an NDE? Your body is dying! I think this helps lend NDEs legitimacy.

Regardless of where NDEs come from, I look at the results. Most of those who've had an NDE report that it transformed their lives. Many end up with heightened psychic sensitivity, spiritual rebirth, a vivid sense of compassion and a compelling need to serve others. In a quantum nutshell, most NDEers have a vivid realization of their consciousness spread across space-time and its true unity with all things. After what may have been a lifetime of frustrating self-ism, they suddenly are over-whelmed by the realization that they are part of the One.

The most mistranslated and misinterpreted passage in the Christian New Testament, at least in the West, has to be Matthew 22:39. "Love your neighbor as yourself," which most of us interpret as "love your neighbor the way you love yourself." But in the original Greek (trans-literated into the Roman alphabet), it says *agapesis ton plaision sou os seauton*: Love your neighbor *because he is* yourself.

After all the terrors I've recalled in this book, after all the physics, the history and the philosophy, I hope that the one thing you'll remember is the simple message that comes from it all: No matter how alone you feel, no mat-ter how desolate, despondent or desperate, you are *never* alone and you are *always* loved. For wherever and when-ever we live in the dazzling infinity and variety of the multiverse, we all are fathers, mothers, brothers, sisters and friends to each other.

And as for "death": In the simple words of St. Julian of Norwich, "In the end, all will be well!"

APPENDICES

Appendix I

Ouija Boards and Séances

Predictions of death

The first and last time I used a Ouija board was in the mid-1960s, when I was still in primary school. My best friend had received one for his birthday, and we tried it in his Connecticut living room one chilly fall day. We were captivated by the moving planchette (the pointing device that spells out words and indicates numbers), and we posed many questions. Finally, we asked when we would die. The board said that my friend would die in 1985.

He did. He was killed at the age of 30 in a scuba-diving accident on September 8 of that year. Although the board pronounced then that I still have a considerable number of years to go, we put away the planchette on that day and we never used the board again.

Today, people frequently ask me about Ouija boards. Often, they announce that they have used them to contact one or another spirit. As a matter of fact, I have an elderly cousin who has used one all her life and believes everything it tells her.

Ouija boards are a method of "divination," a word that literally means "seeking messages from the Gods." Methods of divination have been used throughout history and have included oracles, crystal gazing, reading animal entrails and many others. Though they come in a number of forms, Ouija boards as we know them today are relatively recent. They date only to about 1848, when the famous Fox sisters of New York State started experiencing their alleged communication with spirits, much or all of it reputedly faked.

In the 1890s, William Fuld started mass producing the

modern form of the board as we know it today. Incredibly, big-name game companies produce it today.

When I started my paranormal studies as a high school student in 1970, I immediately began to run into cases that began with people using Ouija boards. Problems included hauntings and oppressions of all kinds, psychological problems of many descriptions and even crime. In the latter case, people would develop such a dependence on the board that they would do whatever it told them. I wrote about one of these cases in my 1998 book *Faces at the Window* ("Trouble from the Ouija Board").

Making matters worse

Another popular practice I've never gotten along with is the séance. In a séance, a group of people led by a medium (the buzzword today is "channeler") gather to contact a spirit or spirits, then ask questions and, frequently, get answers. Various phenomena often occur. Many séances are fakes, some are not.

The general idea is that, by communicating with the allegedly poor, lost spirit that's troubling a person or place, the séance group can help it resolve its problems and "pass over correctly" into the great beyond...rather like a psychiatrist's couch for the "dead."

I never used the practice myself but several investigators I worked with in my salad days did. It seemed obvious to me that when a séance did any good at all, the affect was only temporary. More often than not, there was no change in the situation and sometimes it even got worse.

Why?

Why do Ouija boards and séances cause problems?

Because they both tie into the electromagnetic power of participants' minds to open holes in space-time. Often

156

enough, what comes through those holes are parasitical entities that want to feed off your energy and know just what "buttons" to push to do it. Today, with society characterized by a sort of shared loneliness, I'm convinced that one of these "buttons" is our desperate need for love and friendship. These entities can make people feel special and needed. Well, parasites need you, alright, but not in the way you think.

When predictions take place, it's because whatever is giving them to you is conscious of the quantum probabilities and simply reports one. This is what psychics do, whether they realize it or not. When a prediction comes true, it's simply because it, he, she or they have picked the right probability OR because your own consciousness has "collapsed the wave function" (as theoretical physicists would say) to bring it about.

Whatever comes at you through the board or the séance group may pretend to be your Uncle George and convince you of it. It may even help you for awhile.

But don't be a schmuck! These entities are not your friends!

From the beginning, I've been struck by the tendency of people to believe everything they hear from a Ouija board or at a séance.

Even the Bible warns against this: "Do not trust every spirit," (1 John 4:1). Translated properly from the original Greek, this really says: "Do no *believe* every spirit."

Good advice.

Don't get me wrong: I do believe there are good spirits and plenty of them, especially ancestral ones, but you don't need Ouija boards and séances to seek their help and advice. All you have to do is ask with a pure heart.

Appendix II

The Major Appliances

A landmark discovery in paranormal studies occurred in Britain in 1998, when researchers stumbled on ghost-like phenomena produced by, of all things, a faulty electric fan that was producing very low frequency (VLF) sound waves and creating a "standing wave" in a lab. This wave affected the environment in pretty concrete ways, including the movement and shaking of objects, along with a very basic apparition.

One of the benefits of being a ghost hunter is that one does not expect one's own house to be haunted. But I went out into our upstairs hallway one night in 2001 and ran smack into a wall of electrical energy of the type I find when paranormal phenomena are going on. This went on for over a week. Then, I woke up one night to a shaking bed!

So I took my own advice: I looked for a mundane explanation before assuming that I had a paranormal problem. I scanned the upstairs with my trusty electromagnetic-field meter and, sure enough, I found that the filter pump on my son's aquarium was putting out up to 2,000 gauss, high enough to create a health hazard! I suspected that this filter also was producing VLF sound waves.

We dumped the pump, and all phenomena ceased immediately!

I think that for shaking beds, jangling wine glasses and such, VLF often is the explanation. If you think you have a paranormal situation, first check your appliances and electrical devices to see if they're humming or vibrating. If so, try unplugging them for awhile to see if things quiet down. Of course, VLF waves are too low for us to hear so you may have to experiment.

I think many "ghosts" may well be major appliances!

Footsteps in the Attic

Appendix III

What to Do About Ghosts

If you believe you are having a paranormal problem in your home, here are some steps you should take:

1. Don't jump to conclusions. Always look for everyday explanations for whatever is happening before deciding that you have ghost problems. Consider psychiatric and other health factors as well. (Hearing and seeing things can be a sign of schizophrenia or temporal-lobe epilepsy.) Banging sounds on the walls or in the heating system can have very mundane explanations!

One fascinating explanation for many phenomena are very low-frequency (VLF) sound waves or "standing waves." Trapped in a building, these can cause many of the phenomena associated with ghosts. These waves are inaudible to humans but not to many animals. In humans, they can cause feelings of cold, nervousness, "hair standing up on the back of the neck," minor poltergeist activity and even your basic apparition.

2. Bear in mind that if what we've said about quantum reality is true, every person and every house will experience space-time "glitches" now and then: the occasional shadow seen out of the corner of your eye, or the iron or bit of clothing found now and again where you didn't put it.

Don't let your imagination take over!

Remember, too, that in places where highly traumatic events are occurring in your house in other areas of space-time, you may experience some of the psychic "ripples." Violent deaths, great suffering and other such events that happened or will happen there can affect your reality. Depending on how sensitive you are, you may hear or see things that don't necessarily mean that your house is "haunted" or that you or other household members are the targets of negative entities.

Nevertheless, it's always best to be on the safe side and to do what's suggested below.

It's when these "glitches" begin to rule your everyday life, when you feel threatened by them and/or when entities begin to clearly manifest and interact with you or your family that you have a paranormal problem.

3. If you conclude that you do have such a situation, realize that you and/or one or more family members probably are part of the problem. Consciously or unconsciously, people in troubled houses always have a part in causing and/or feeding the phenomena. So you need to find what you're doing that's introducing or encouraging negative energy.

4. Then you need to stop it and bring in positive energy to replace it. I find this always eases the situation and often cures it.

Examples of negative energy: using Ouija boards or other occult practices that "open the door" to parasites, negative feelings among those who live in the house (fights, grudges, financial strains, etc.) and the extreme depression or anxiety of you or any other household member.

5. Part of bringing in this positive energy is fostering good feeling, humor, love and other unifying and uplifting factors in your household. Also, good physical exercise and developing healthy interests outside the home will help.

This is always good for a household, whether you have paranormal problems or not.

6. If you do encounter an "orb," entity or other manifestation, try to avoid fear or anger. If it really is a negative entity, this will deny it the negative energy it subsists on. As a matter of fact, always try to send out feelings of love, compassion and peace.

7. In general, however, do not give these entities atten-

Footsteps in the Attic

tion. Do not try to communicate with them: *They are not your friends!* Don't try to get "chummy" and don't convince yourself to feel comfortable with them around, even if they seem "friendly." Instead, concentrate on fostering positive energy among the household members.

8. Anytime you are afraid, pray in whatever way is comfortable for you. Visualize yourself, other household members and your home engulfed in a peaceful, positive white light. This will "take the wind" out of a negative manifestation by strengthening you instead of it.

9. This is not advice you often hear in the Western Hemisphere but, when you are afraid, you can call upon your *good* ancestors (not the horse thieves or mad monarchs) to help protect you and your home. I find that this is a very powerful practice! Each of us is the sum of our ancestors, no matter how far back they go. We are part of them and they are part of us. Since there really is no death, these loved ones are always in some parallel world and there is a bond between you and them. Many are in a position to help.

Call especially on particular loved ones you have known, a beloved grandmother, for example. If you are fortunate enough to have a picture of the person, put it in a prominent place in your home or carry it in your pocket or purse. These people will manifest as quiet and loving presences, and some may be protecting you already. Their presence is a far cry from the cold, sterile and sometimes violent presence of parasites and tulpas.

10. If you belong to a particular religion, praying and using "sacramentals" and sacred objects such as icons, your scriptures or holy water can help. Strange to say, beware of calling in clergy unless you are very sure they can be trusted. Believe it or not, very few of them are trained in how to deal with these phenomena and if they don't know what they're doing they can complicate the situation.

Footsteps in the Attic

GLOSSARY

Apparition
—The visible form of a ghost

Divination, divining
—An ancient practice that uses one or another instruments (including mirrors, pendula, Ouija boards, dowsing rods, etc.) to learn information not available to the physical senses.

Electronic Voice Phenomena (EVP)
—Believed to be the recording of paranormal voices on audio equipment. The author doubts its validity in many cases, but believes that some instances may be examples of contact with parallel universes.

Ghost
—A lifeform, human or otherwise, perceived at the conjunction of two or more parallel universes.

The Multiverse
—In theoretical physics, the totality of parallel universes that compose ultimate reality.

Near Death Experience (NDE)
—For most people who undergo it as the brain dies or is otherwise traumatized, the experience of passing through a tunnel toward a light, at the end of which may be deities or loved ones.

Orb
—A ball or globule of light often seen at haunted sites or in paranormal photography. There is disagreement on what they are.

Out-of-the-Body Experience (OBE)
—An experience in which the consciousness seems to be outside the physical body.

Parasites
—As used in this book, intelligent lifeforms from other parts of the multiverse who get into our universe and

Footsteps in the Attic

feed off humans, geotechnic energies and other sources of electricity. They are interpreted as ghosts.

Poltergeist

—From two German words meaning "noisy spirit." A mischievous or violent manifestation of a parasitical ghost.

Psychic or Paranormal Photography

—A phenomenon in which ghostly streaks, faces, people or other attributes appear on photographic negatives or prints. Usually, the photographer is unaware of these "extras" in the photos until they are developed. Also refers to the conscious projection of mental images onto photographic film.

Space-Time

—In modern physics, the concept of space and time as one and the same. It derives from Einstein's vision of the physical universe, which is based on Hermann Minkowski's geometric system.

Time Slip or Time Displacement

—Contact with past or future events, people or places through a conjunction of parallel universes. The author often refers to these as "ghosts from elsewhen."

Tulpa

—An entity believed to be created by the concentration of one or more human minds. More likely a parasitical ghost that feeds on the concentration, then manifests. When visible, it can take the form of a human or animal.

Very Low Frequency Sound Waves (VLF)

—These can create standing waves in buildings that may produce basic ghost phenomena. VLF sources may include faulty appliances, stereo subwoofers and even wind passing over a house.

INDEX

M

Footsteps in the Attic

The Author

PAUL F. ENO has been an investigator of paranormal phenomena for over 30 years. A prize-winning journalist who has done postgraduate work in psychology, philosophy, history, theology, literature and law, he has a special love for New England history and folklore. Mr. Eno is a former news editor at **The Providence Journal** *and a former managing editor of Observer Publications in Smithfield, R.I. Articles by him have appeared in* **Yankee, Fate, Pursuit, American History Illustrated,** *other national magazines in America and Britain and nearly every Rhode Island newspaper. Mr. Eno now works as a freelance writer and editor from his Rhode Island home.*

Also by Paul F. Eno

(From New River Press)
Faces at the Window (1998)
The Best of Times (1992)

(From Oxford University Press, London)
"William Blackstone"
in American National Biography

(From Pamphlet Publications, Chicago)
The Occult (1977)*
Preventive Medicine for the Occult
(1979)*

(coming from New River Press)
Rhode Island: A Genial History (2003)
(with Glenn Laxton)

*out of print

Footsteps in the Attic